ROOTED
and Established

SUSAN NOEL LAURITA

ROOTED
and Established

A Story of Love and Resilience

XULON PRESS

Xulon Press
555 Winderley Pl, Suite 225
Maitland, FL 32751
407.339.4217
www.xulonpress.com

xulon
PRESS

Unless otherwise indicated, Scripture quotations taken from the Holy Bible, New International Version (NIV). Copyright © 1973, 1978, 1984, 2011 by Biblica, Inc.™. Used by permission. All rights reserved.

Paperback ISBN-13: 979-8-86850-339-9
eBook ISBN-13: 979-8-86850-340-5

To my family, Larry Laurita, Andrea Laurita, and Amanda Hall who spent countless hours reviewing and suggesting, and who love me well.

To John Espy, a friend of a friend, who generously added his professional eye.

To my grandparents, Frank and Mae Noel, whose example I cherish, and who I hope to spend more time with when this life is done.

To couples everywhere who may find life difficult and wonder if you will make it. If you both decide to, you will.

And I pray that you, being rooted and established in love, may have the power together with all the saints, to grasp how wide and long and high and deep is the love of Christ.

Ephesians 3:17b
New International Version

Table of Contents

Author's Note

Some people grow up knowing their grandparents. I didn't.

Luckily, one of my aunts, Jennie Noel Weeks, convinced her parents to write their own stories which she compiled and bound for later generations. That volume is called **80 Years in America** and, from what I can gather, she had enough volumes printed for every child and grandchild who was alive at the time. She was also one of the people instrumental in getting the history of my grandmother's family together in **Roberts Family: Connecticut to California**, and in compiling a genealogy complete with copies of other relevant documents in **Book of Remembrance: Noel and Roberts Master Pedigree**.

As I read through these books and others, what emerged was a story of resilience and steadfastness that I couldn't ignore. Just two generations removed, but over 100 years earlier, my grandparents lived in a time, in cultures I can only try to imagine. In their stories I found wealthy plantation life and living in a tent. I found covered wagons and learning to drive a car. There is hard work, hard play, forbidden love, faith, and skepticism. A Navajo uprising that had the whole nation on edge brought both the U.S. Army and the Navajo leaders literally into my grandparents' home. They lived through a flood so historic it has yet to be repeated, a pandemic, and the Great Depression.

It is a story worth telling. It is a legacy worth embracing.

Respectfully,
Susan Noel Laurita

P.S. For the sake of clarity, I have called my grandmother Mae throughout the book. Her name is Mary Eliza Roberts Noel. But since her mother, one of her daughters, and her sister-in-law are also named Mary, I used Mae, one of her nicknames, to avoid confusion.

Spelling of the Navajo names varies. My grandfather's spelling was often phonetic. I went with the form I found most frequently except in places where I include a direct quotation.

Quotations are given just as they appear in the original. And the curious little numbers you see after quotations refer to the resources listed at the very end.

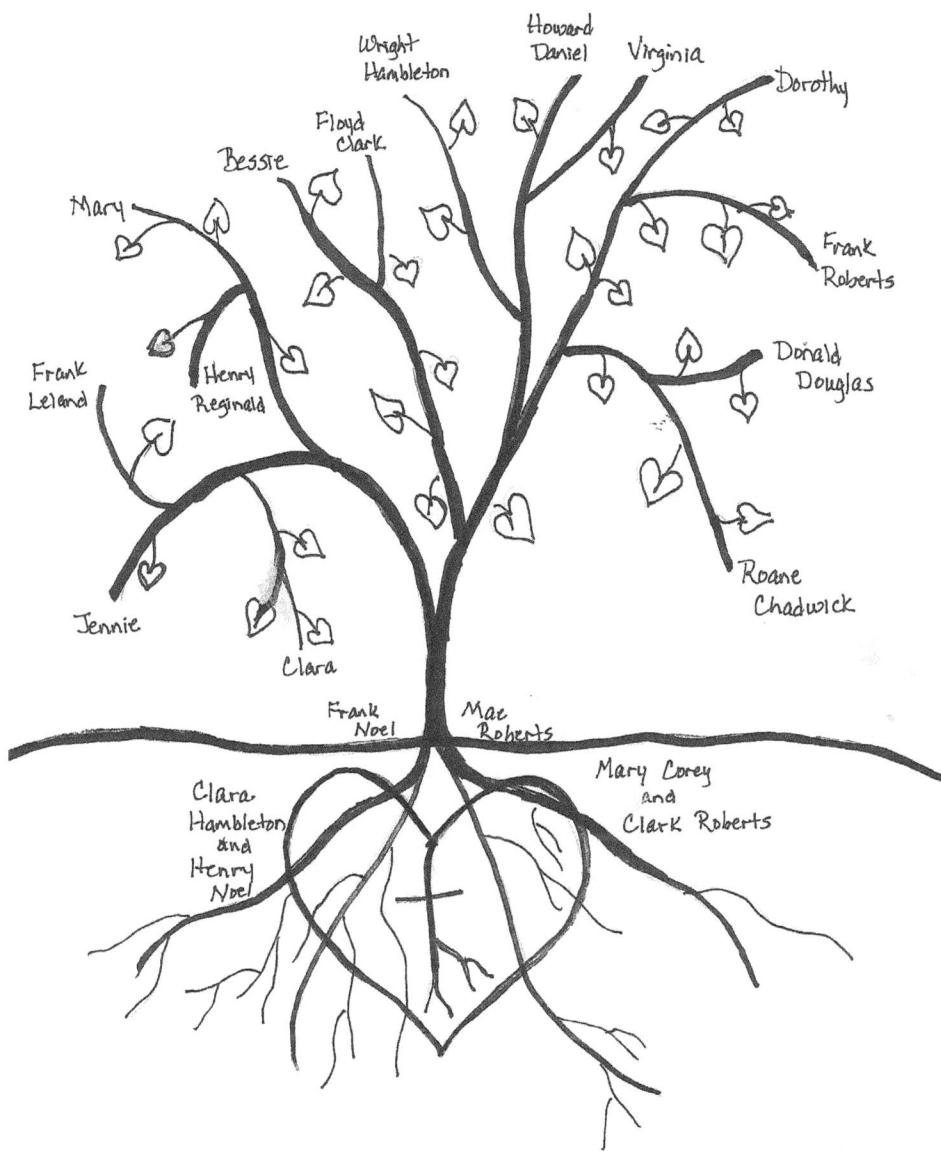

Family Tree
Source: Susan Laurita

CHAPTER 1:

1880 - Answering the Call

"Mae, we're stopping here for a little bit. Hop down now and see that your brothers have enough water for them and the horses. Etta will help you with the buckets." Mae happily hopped down from the buckboard, pleased with the prospect of stretching her legs and helping out while her mother tended to the babies. Her parents had told her they were in the middle of an important adventure, and she was excited to be a part of it.

In 1862, President Abraham Lincoln signed into law the Homestead Act, designed to populate vast parts of the country that were uncharted and to give thousands the opportunity to own the home they might not otherwise be able to afford. All you had to do was pack up everything you owned, head west through an unknown and sometimes dangerous wilderness, find a spot you liked, and start to build your home. If you were the head of household, women and freed slaves included, at least 21 years of age, and had plans to become a loyal American citizen, you could claim up to 160 acres of land free and clear. (1)

Mae's uncle, Howard Corey, and his brothers jumped at the chance, with Howard securing his parcel of 160 acres in 1876.

Homestead Act certificate
Source: (2)

Three years later, in 1879, John Taylor, president of the Church of Jesus Christ of Latter-Day Saints, called for church volunteers to venture out and settle parts of southeastern Utah, southwestern Colorado, and northern New Mexico. As the membership spread out, he reasoned, the church would also spread.

Howard's sister, Mary, and her husband, Clark Roberts, were among those who answered the call. They packed up their six children, left their farm, rounded up their livestock, and prepared to join a group of people heading south. One of their children was an almost four-year-old girl named Mary or Mae. She was my grandmother.

On September 1, 1880, their wagon train of about 100 wagons set out on the dangerous trek south from Mona, Utah to an unknown future. Clark drove the wagon full of supplies. Mary followed in the buggy with the younger children. Two of their sons, Howard and Orville, ages eight and 10, drove the cattle and horses on the side. And a young Native woman by the name of Etta Lewellen rode with them to help with cooking and the children.

Family members who didn't come with them were still supportive, still believed this would be an exciting start to something wonderful. Mary's mother made sure they had plenty of beef jerky for the trip. Clark's brother, Bolivar Roberts, who led the Pony Express, supplied them with a four-horse team to pull the wagon of supplies.

Gold Miners Heading West Wagon Train, 1899

Heading West
Source:Stock.com/bauhaus1000

They were guided by two men. Brother John Allen, Jr. was their captain and would be the one to scout ahead for water, grassland for the animals, and the best path forward. Brother Rasmussen was the chaplain. It was Brother Rasmussen who called, "All ye, come to prayer," every morning before heading out and every evening before retiring for bed. The wagons would form a circle and he would wait patiently until everyone was accounted for and kneeling in their family groups. "Brother Clark, will you pray for us this time please?"

"Dear Father God, we thank you for this day and …"

By today's standards, it was very slow going, desperately slow.

By the end of October, almost two months and over 300 miles later, they reached Mancos Hill in Colorado. The snow there was about 18 inches deep, too deep to move on with wagons loaded with supplies. They rested for a few days while the sun warmed the ground. Some of their oxen saw their chance to wander away from the main group and were soon nowhere to be found. So, when the wagon train began to move on, the Coreys, Roberts, and others stayed behind to help round up the wayward livestock. That done, they headed in the direction the other wagons had taken.

Before they caught up with the larger group, they heard about a railroad company that was paying good money to those who would help clear a space for a railroad. It was worth checking out. Winter was going to slow them down anyway. They headed along the San Juan River in New Mexico, found the railroad camp, and decided to stop and work for a while before heading out again in the spring. There were no deadlines. They would take it one day at a time and keep going when they could.

The first thing they needed was a place to stay through the fall and winter. Mae's family built a one-room cabin with a roof covered in dirt for insulation. Canvas covers from the wagon were used to let in the light. Bunks were placed around the walls with a fireplace at one end and a cookstove at the other.

It was a grueling winter. The men and older boys had to blast a hill down, cut trees, and drag great blocks of ice from the river. The girls and women maintained their daily routines: meals prepared, animals cared for, snow melted for water, clothes washed by hand, and at least the six children in the Roberts family to care for. Who knows how many more children were there from the other families? Etta took a job with the railroad camp and spent her days there. With her help no longer available, everyone had plenty to do.

The children seemed unworried by the lack of any comforts they had left behind. They trusted their parents to take care of them, as children do, and woke up every morning knowing they were together and in the middle of a great adventure. The older children had some chores, gathering wood and hauling water. The younger children helped where they could, but also enjoyed being free to run and play, no longer cooped up in the wagons.

There was no recognized law and order at the railroad camp. It was up to each man, woman, and child to live the best way they could. Situations could get pretty violent at times, but the Roberts and Corey families went about their business and were normally untouched by trouble. Normally, but not always.

One Sunday morning, as the Coreys were going to the Roberts camp, they found a Mexican man tied to a tree. He had stab wounds all over his body and was nearly frozen. Realizing he was still alive, they cut him down and carried him to the back of a nearby store. There, they tended his wounds the best way they could as they prayed for his recovery.

There is no indication that they ever knew why he was there, or who stabbed him and tied him to the tree. We do know that he recovered.

It wasn't until the spring of 1881 that the Roberts family arrived in Mancos, CO and caught up with the other families from their wagon train. What a reunion! They spent the next few days catching up with each other, laughing at any missteps their friends had made, marveling at how well some had made it through, and commenting on how the little ones were growing. Finally, they turned their thoughts to the future. Should they settle here? Should they keep moving on? Joseph Smith, among other men, urged them to stay. Some of their group had already started to establish themselves here, he reasoned. They would be welcomed among friends, and it looked like this area was going to be growing. The Roberts agreed to stay, happy to be at the end of their trek and part of something bigger than themselves.

It was a short stay.

Within a few months, they got word that Mary's mother was gravely ill. If Mary wanted to see her mother again, she should come now. So, they packed up the children and headed back to Provo, Utah, retracing the country they had just come through. It would be almost a year before Mary and the children returned.

Mary's Journal entries (condensed):

Tuesday, September 6, 1881: After a very pleasant sojourn here of about three months, we are off again.... This time, with a yearning and a sick heart, to see a noble and worn-out mother. May God grant that I shall find her better than I fear; that she may live many years yet to bless the lives of her children, for whom she has given hers; and may I prove worthy to be associated with her hereafter. Left Mancos at 12 o'clock and camped near the Deloros [River].

Wednesday, September 7th: moved to the other side of the river and camped..... This is beautiful country; the campground is shaded with large cottonwood trees and nicely carpeted with grass. Clark and I fished some, ate lunch on the bank of the river and went to the wagon without any fish. The boys caught some.

Thursday, September 8th was out early and got to cross canyon late in the evening.

Friday, September 9th: Out at daylight and camped at a small spring a few miles north of Pinte. Have been most sick all day. The road was very rough.

Saturday, September 10th: Got to Lisbon early, ate supper, and drove some distance by moonlight. Mrs. White got an Indian scare. She is very timid.

Sunday, September 11th: Started early, climbed a fearful hill, then drove for some time in a forest of cedars and nooned at Hyota Creek, filled the water barrels and drove about eight miles, camped at the foot of a flint hill. There was the greatest variety of flint I ever saw. There was quite an excitement raised by Mrs. White by a dog barking.

Monday, September 12th: Reached Cain Springs early, most famished and worn out; wrote to Mary Corey [sister-in-law] – sold Dave [horse].

Tuesday, September 13th: Traveled over the worst roads I ever saw, on account of the wash leaving rocks high and bare. Then climbed a fearful hill, not so bad as in the fall. Mrs. Garner's horse broke his legs. We reached Grand Valley by dark.

Wednesday, September 14th: Laid over to see how many horses we had here. Ate watermelons.

Thursday, September 15th: Was quite sick with a cold. Brother Wilson called on us. He is so changed by the death of his boys.

Friday, September 16th: I am much better today but have a dreadful cough and can scarcely speak loud. Crossed Grand River with the blessings of God in safety. Dragged slowly through the sand and over the hill to Court House Rock.

Saturday, September 17th: reached the holes in the rocks by noon; this is a wonderful construction of nature, there are several large holes in the solid rock along the ravine. They are like large wash bowls that hold several barrels each of rainwater that flows into them from each side, which is a great blessing to the famished travelers. We ate a few bites and rode on into the night; the wind is blowing.

Sunday, September 18th: Started on without breakfast, no wood to cook with! Drove fifteen miles and crossed Green River. Cooked and ate our breakfast with relish. Went to the store to mail some cards. Hitched up and drove on till very late looking for grass in vain. Bought some corn at an R.R. camp; drove to a high bank where the horses stopped, and Clark concluded to tie up till morning. Oh! This fearful desert!

Monday, September 19th: *Started again without breakfast; drove three miles and camped on Cottonwood, a small but pretty stream that trinkles over large black sandstone rocks, ate breakfast then drove on to Big Hole in the Rock.*

Tuesday, September 20th: *Got quite a moderate start this morning which gave me time to look around some. These huge ridges of sand rock that are washed by every storm look quite grand. . We nooned at what they call little holes in the rocks, but it is far from the fact. This is the most chasm of rocks I ever saw or dreamed of; it is miles in length and stores the water it gathers 30 to 50 feet below its banks. It took some time to water the stock, so I walked all over the torn hills but saw nothing that I recognize as rare or valuable. Camped at Buck Horn Flat.*

Wednesday, September 21st: *Reached Cottonwood Creek. I washed, the wind blew and prevented me from leaving camp. It put me out of humor.*

Thursday, September 22nd: *Climbed fearful canyon, camped near the head of it. Goodbye Castle Valley: May Heaven pity you, I do.*

Friday, September 23rd: *Traveled in a new snowstorm all day and camped in it at night. It is very cold.*

Saturday, September 24th: *We have traveled stormily today. Passed many familiar scenes that brought up pleasant memories of our last fall's trip. Camped on Gooseberry. Very cold.*

Sunday, September 25th: *Went down the grade and camped at a place near North Bend. Met some old friends.*

Monday, September 26th: *Clark went to North Bend with Nielsen, met Bolivar. Hurried back to make a short drive; passed through an Indian village in Thistle Valley. Very cold.*

Tuesday, September 27th: *Reached home – Oh! How timidly I entered the house not knowing how I should find Ma, but she was so she could talk to me* *and so highly appreciative of my* company *that I feel paid already for my trip. Met Nellie [sister] and family whom I had not seen for three years which was no small pleasure. Oh! Merciful Father, help me to comfort and bless my mother.* (3)

God granted her prayer. Mary's mother passed away in December. She and the children stayed with relatives through the winter and Clark returned home to prepare a place for them. Their dream of a new future, though postponed, was still alive.

One Journal Entry Going Back

Tuesday, February 28, 1882: I took leave once more of the home of my child-hood, with all its dear associations and loved graves of my mother and sister. When we moved to this place, I was about nine years old. There were eight of us children, poor and destitute, yet tenderly attached to each other and shared our troubles cheerfully, always looking forward to a time when God in his mercy would lift the cloud of darkness that shadowed our financial pathway and grant us the privilege of storing our minds with the rich treasures of knowledge. A thirst that our mother had in her untiring efforts inspired us with. (3)

There was no compulsory education for children at that time. Families did the best they could to pass on the knowledge they thought was important to their children. Few had enough money for private tutors or time to dedicate to home schooling children. Some families believed it just wasn't important. There was some discussion about developing a public education system, and some cities in the East had them. But it would be decades before education was required. According to Mary's journal entry, her mother thought of education as a "treasure." I am grateful.

Their trip back, in March, was to be by train. It was five unpleasant days of Mary and six active children being crammed into close quarters, wondering how long it would be before they could see their father again. But compared to the three weeks it had taken them to get there, Mary understood it was blessedly short in comparison. She was grateful for the five days, and she was looking forward to seeing Clark, settling down, and establishing their new home.

When they arrived, Clark met them at the train station and took them to a two-room log house. It had a dirt floor, a fireplace in one corner, and a small cookstove in the other corner, very much like the temporary shelter they had near the railroad camp. It was nothing like the homes Mary had just left. There was no electricity, no bathroom, and no running water.

The house was on the bank of Chicken Creek surrounded by cottonwood, pinon trees, and lots of wildflowers. For the children, days were spent hauling water to be used in the house, collecting firewood, exploring the river, gathering nuts and berries when they were in season, playing in the trees with children from nearby families, and sailing little boats in the creek.

There were two small rooms for eight people who lived simply, loved each other, and trusted God. It was there they learned to say their prayers and where their father took them in his arms and baptized them in the creek. Mae would later say she couldn't imagine loving a place any more than she loved this little home.

They lived there for eight years, until 1890.

CHAPTER 2:

1892 - Remembering Paynefield

Paynefield
Source: Frank R. Noel collection

Dr. Henry R. Noel and his wife, Clara, had six children: Henry, Edmund, Frank (my grandfather), Wright, Hambleton, and their sister Bessie. Unlike my grandmother, Frank Leland Noel, was being raised on his family's sprawling 1,000–acre plantation near Tappahannock, Virginia. Known as Paynefield, it was a fairly typical plantation in the late 1800s. The main house had two fireplaces for heat, one on each end of the house. There was a separate building for the kitchen and root cellar. Other buildings were for storing corn and meat. Still others were for horses, cows, turkeys, ducks, and chickens. There was a carriage house. Several cabins that once housed slaves were now occupied by families, both black and white, who worked on the plantation. Some owned their homes. Some rented. There were lots of trees for the five boys to climb. Fruit trees, nut trees, and shade trees were watered by irrigation from the nearby Rappahannock River. Acres of vegetables, berries, hay, corn, and cotton contributed to making Paynefield nearly self-sufficient. Solomon Bogues took care of the gardens and meat. Henry Fells, an expert cobbler and harness maker, was another indispensable part of their lives. When the children were young, a woman they called Aunt Patience, who was in charge of the children, trusted the boys to roam and play during a good part of the day.

Aunt Patience with little Bessie just before Bessie died. Source: **80 Years in America** (4)

Their father, Dr. Henry R. Noel, was diagnosed early on with consumption, a deadly disease that caused him to run a fever and be frequently wracked with coughing fits that brought up blood. Since it is contagious, he spent most of his time isolated in his bedroom. The children were not allowed to have direct contact with him at all. They barely knew him, only that he was himself a doctor who had served the Confederate army, that he loved them, and that he was very sick. Clara, their mother, established the habit of visiting the children in the nursery every day around suppertime. Aunt Patience made sure they were all washed and ready so they could spend the next few hours telling stories, talking about the day, making plans, and saying their prayers. Those were precious times.

Dr. Henry Noel died when he was only 40. Frank was five. Their little sister, Bessie, died soon after that.

The law allowing women to own property was slow in reaching Virginia. Other states had already passed laws that said married women could own property. Many of them included a caveat that also said they were not allowed to *manage* the property. It would take a man to do that. Eventually states started passing laws for "equal economy" for women, but sometimes it only applied to married women. Henry Noel was a doctor, and he knew he was dying. So, with the ability of his wife to manage the plantation after his death uncertain, he left everything to his wife's brother, Edward Hamilton. It was common practice at the time to entrust property to a concerned male relative in hopes he would look after the widow and orphans.

Henry's trust in Uncle Ed was well placed. Although he lived in the city of Baltimore, he made it a point to visit now and then, to be sure the plantation was still running smoothly, to take care of any needs that came up, and to ensure the land was being put to good use.

A thousand acres is a lot of land, and Frank would have liked to have had more time there with his mother, and much less time in a job he couldn't enjoy.

But I'm getting ahead of myself.

A teacher was hired for the Noel boys, and then breakfast was at 8 a.m. and school started at 9. The lunch break lasted from noon to 1 p.m. and then there were two more hours of school. Supper was at 6 p.m. and, for the older boys, homework was from 7 to 8 p.m. That schedule lasted until Frank was 12 years old. Then he and his older two brothers went to public school in Tappahannock.

On those school mornings, the brothers took turns going to the barn, getting the horse and buggy ready and bringing it to the main house. Then they had breakfast, drove six miles to school in the buggy, did their studies, drove six miles home, put up the horse and buggy, brought in wood chips for the fire, had dinner, spent time with Mother, then fell into bed to do it again the next day. While Mae Roberts and her siblings were enjoying significantly less structured days in the two-room cabin on Chicken Creek, Frank and his brothers found their days to be very full.

You would think they had no extra time left to get into trouble on school days. But, as it turned out, some boys have a mischievous streak.

Memories

"Sh-hh." Frank held his finger in front of his lips and winked at his seatmate. He leaned forward and placed a tack, sharp side up, on the seat of his classmate who was working on a math problem at the front of the class. "Ouch!" yelled the unwary classmate when he sat down. "Frank Noel, come here this instant!" bellowed the schoolmaster. Someone snitched. Frank went to the front of the class and got his hands smacked with a ruler while other boys giggled. Then, after school, he fought with the boy who told on him. The memory of it made Frank smile years later. Harmless fun. He would do it again if he had the chance.

The brothers always learned to expect consequences for their misdeeds. Their mother was loving but just, so each of the boys was rewarded for his good deeds and paid for his misdeeds. It kept her busy, like the afternoon their cat, Snow, fought with a possum. Frank found the possum in the hollow trunk of a tree. When he came near, the possum pretended to be dead, so he put a stick in and wrapped the possum's tail around it. His brother helped him carry it home and put it in a barrel. Eventually, the boys had the idea of tying the possum's long tail with the long grey tail of their cat. They put each one in a burlap sack, tied their tails together, threw them over the clothesline, then took off the burlap sacks, and stood back. What a fight! Between the large mouth and teeth of the possum and the sharp claws of the cat, the fur went flying and both animals were soon covered in blood. All the brothers stood there cheering. They tried hard to be quiet; but how could they with a fight like that? "Boys!" Clara shouted. Five boys froze. "Frank, cut those brutes down!"

That particular prank cost Frank a switching, a lecture, and an hour of hoeing weeds in the sun. His possum had to go to a local family that was happy to add it to their stew pot. But the memory of that, too, still made him smile decades later. Frank said trouble seemed to come easy for him, but sometimes the prank was worth the punishment. "Hard work never hurts anybody," he thought.

Occasionally, they would have visitors from the city, or one of their uncles would come by for a few days. On one of these visits, Uncle Ed saw a dog get into the chicken yard and eat a nest full of eggs. He called for his rifle and killed the dog. The dog's owner was not too happy about it but decided to voice his displeasure from his own side of the fence. No sense making more trouble when the other guy already had his gun.

Uncle Ed, for his part, started thinking of a way to keep dogs out of the henhouse. Sending them a big dog, he reasoned, would discourage other dogs from eating their eggs.

So, not too many weeks later, a steamer from Tappahannock brought a black Newfoundland to protect the chickens and children of Paynefield. Leo had a white star on his chest, weighed 120 pounds, and was both gentle and an efficient guardian. The boys loved him immediately. Clara quickly learned to love Leo too and felt safe with him walking by her side. She learned that Leo was not only faithful, but smart. One word from her out in the field and he would bring the milk cows to the barn to be milked. A definite advantage.

One of Frank's favorite memories was racing Leo and his brothers to the pond and spending time swimming with him. Most of the boys learned to swim by holding onto Leo's thick coat or tail. And anytime Frank had an errand to run, he would take Leo with him. If the place they were visiting also had dogs, there was no question that Leo could hold his own. Sometimes Frank would egg him on, just to watch him win.

There was one time when Frank and his older brother, Henry, headed home from the swimming hole and came upon a wild boar. The boar was big and ready for a fight. It started charging toward the boys and they lost no time scuttling up a tree. The boar couldn't climb, but he wasn't leaving either. What were they going to do? How long would they have to stay up in that tree?

When Frank remembered they had left Leo at the swimming hole, he called to him, and Leo was there in no time. He saw the boar, heard Frank holler "Get him!" and rushed right in. It was a risky move.

Wild boars have been known to kill any dogs who challenged them. And this boar was more than ready to fight. He was big and strong and used to getting his way. But once Leo had a good grip on his ear, he slowed down a

16

bit. The boys climbed out of the tree, picked up sticks, and started beating the boar on the back. Once it started squealing, they knew they had him. They called Leo off, held him back, and the boar ran away as fast as his little legs would take him.

In the winter the pond would partially freeze, and the boys would stake out a spot to do some ice fishing. On one occasion, they took Leo with them and tied him up at the edge of the pond. Frank had built a little platform in the water to get closer to the fish. The trouble started when he noticed a big water moccasin circling his little platform. Now water moccasins are very aggressive, very poisonous snakes. They are definitely not something you want circling around you. Frank threw his line over the snake and jerked it up. The hook caught the snake in the middle of its back, and made it very angry. Frank fought to keep the snake out of reach as the snake writhed on the hook. When the other boys started whooping and jumping up and down, Leo couldn't stand it. He broke loose and jumped onto the pond. Now, in addition to watching what the snake was doing, Frank had to lift it high enough that Leo couldn't reach it. One bite and the big dog would be gone. Finally, one of the other boys got Leo back to shore and tied him up again. Frank brought the snake to shore, and the boys beat it to death with sticks.

Another of Frank's favorite memories was the fox hunts. Most of the big plantations had them. Ten to 12 men would show up on their best horses with a couple of hunting dogs apiece. One of the men would have a horn and he would signal when the hunt was to begin. Then the excitement would start. Foxes running literally for dear life, dogs barking wildly when they tracked the scent, horses chasing over the land, jumping over split rail fences, splashing through streams; it all created quite a rush for young Frank and his brothers. They were too young to join those hunts, but they couldn't miss the excitement, or the fun afterward.

In that culture, even the younger boys had opportunities to hunt. Turkeys, rabbits, squirrels, ducks, and a variety of other birds were all fair game, and they loved it. They had their own guns at an early age, and they knew how to use them.

Frank remembers his muzzle-loading shotgun. He would put in a measure of powder, then a wad of paper, and pack it down with a ramrod. Then he would add the shot, another wad of paper, and pack it down again. He then lifted the trigger, put on a cap, and carefully let the trigger down again. Different sizes of buckshot were used depending on the size of the prey. Small buckshot was used for birds. A slightly larger buckshot was used for small animals and turkeys.

Hunting was something Frank loved all his life.

One of his most memorable hunts was a turkey hunt with his older brother Henry. Henry had gotten pretty good at making a wild turkey call. So the boys positioned themselves behind a fence in a place where they knew turkeys liked to gather. Henry made his call, and a big tom turkey came running in their direction. Still crouched down, Henry continued to call. Before they knew it, the tom turkey flew up and landed on the fence just above their heads. Each boy just reached up and grabbed a leg and pulled. The turkey was surprised and put up a good fight to get free, but it didn't help. The brothers fought until they could tie him up and get him stuffed in a bag. It was probably the easiest meal they ever brought home. There wasn't even a need for a gun. Just Henry's turkey call, quick reflexes, and a big sack.

As they grew, of course, they took on chores. Frank, being the middle child, always felt like he got the chores doled out to the older boys **and** the younger boys. It was frustrating at the time. But, as a result, he became capable and strong.

In addition to their chores, when Frank was 10 years old, he and brothers Wright and Edmund were given an acre of land each to cultivate however they wanted. Anything they grew on their acre was theirs and any profit they could get from it was also theirs. That hope was a good motivator.

Corn and wheat were favorites. The only trouble was that their ox, Spot, was also very fond of corn. Spot was a lot bigger, a lot stronger, and a lot more determined than all of the boys put together. Nevertheless, Spot couldn't eat ALL the corn. What was left was put into barrels to be taken to the grist mill a couple of miles away. They would take in five barrels of wheat and five barrels of corn. While the miller was grinding it into flour, the boys would fish in the pond near the water wheel that powered the mill.

Well into adulthood, some of Frank's favorite memories from those early years included a steamboat trip his mother took him on, stockings hung over the fireplace at Christmas, and a particular fox hunt over the Christmas of 1885. Through it all, he remembered doing everything with his brothers: working, playing, hunting, fishing, climbing, fighting, praying, and lots of laughing.

Years folded happily into years. Their mother, Clara, taught them the difference between right and wrong and that you reaped what you sowed. She dispensed justice fairly and calmed their fears when they needed it. She taught them that they had an honorable name, and they were to be sure it was honorable when their time came to lay it down. And she taught them to trust in God to take care of their needs. He had promised to care for the widows and orphans, and that included them. Her sons hoed the garden, cut wood, fed and milked the cows, planted their own parcels of ground, and, when they got older, they got jobs. She believed in them, she relied on them, and they all knew it. All the brothers were fiercely devoted to their mother.

Thinking about those years made Frank miss her terribly.

Orphaned

When Frank was 15, he was sent to Aberdeen Academy in King and Queen County, Virginia, where he and three of his brothers graduated.

Frank was 17, and still in school, when his mother contracted consumption and his whole world changed. She had to travel occasionally to climates the doctors thought would be good for her condition. So the four older brothers took jobs in Baltimore, where their uncles lived. That was the beginning of a strange new life for them. The uncles were good to them, but they were country boys now living and working in the big city, and it was a bit of an adjustment to say the least.

Hambleton, the youngest, was still at Paynefield. Henry went to Virginia Military Academy in Atlanta. Wright went to work as an accountant. Edmund eventually lived and worked with their Uncle John, another of their mother's brothers, at the Hambleton Bank. Frank lived with Uncle John too, and, after graduating, worked at the offices of the West Virginia Central Railroad. He would walk down the street with Uncle John amid lots of carriages and horses. His uncle wore a top hat and cane, and the trams would stop for him to cross. Frank thought his uncle must be very important. They would eat lunch in town, but dinner was at home… and it was all very proper. It meant white cuffs, a black coat, a white starched collar, and sitting properly from 5 p.m. until 7 p.m. listening to stories of the day. To Frank, who was used to more freedom on the plantation, it was torture.

The next few years were difficult; but Frank's main concern was for Mother. They wrote letters back and forth, but it wasn't the same as being with her. She tried to keep her letters upbeat. She would tell him how much she missed her sons and a little about the effort to help her lungs improve.

They didn't. Frank was 19 when she died. Among the things most precious to him were those letters. One of them he kept folded up and in his back pocket.

How was he supposed to know what to do without his mother's guiding hand? He was 19 and parentless. He barely remembered his father. When Mother died, he lost his rock, his compass. Despite his habit of getting into trouble, he had always known she would set him on the right path.

Which path should he take now? His home, Paynefield, would soon be sold. He was suddenly feeling very much like an orphan. His chest tightened. Paynefield. He had never called anywhere else home. He was raised there. Heck, his father was raised there. He had a place now with his uncle, but he couldn't imagine calling it home. Frank couldn't help but long for the earlier days. He felt stuck.

He pulled the letter out of his pocket and started to read it again.

March 30, 1891

My dear Frank,

To-day has been so bright – and I have had a nice ride with Wright for my driver. He has enjoyed his visit home ever so much, seems as happy as a bird and will go back on Wednesday. He has not been very well, or I should not have approved such a long holiday.

Your bright letters dear Son give me the greatest pleasure and I feel so glad you and Edmund keep so well. I can trust both of you to do your best about your work. You have been brave good boys and made me love you more than ever if that is possible....

A short letter from Henry this morning tells he is well and well satisfied. He seems to be happier as all of his letters have reached him at last. I do so hope all may go well with him.

I was surprised indeed that Bro. John has drawn out of the Bank. What will be the name of the firm now? I think he is altogether right, but the others will miss him sadly. How is Uncle Ed?

Do not worry about my moving. I have not begun to plan for it yet for I shall not go until it gets really warm. I do not think there will be any hurry and I shall consider my health first. So do not worry dear.

All will come out right, I trust. We have the promise of the God of the widow and the fatherless. Truly we can trust Him when He has cared for us so kindly. . ..

Uncle John will do what he thinks best. He has been a kind friend to you.

We shall all feel better and brighter when the weather settles and must all be brave until it does.

Use your evenings for improvement. Remember how young you are and how much you have to learn.

> *My warmest love to Edmund and write whenever you can.*
> *Your devoted Mother*
> *Private collection*

Frank held the letter a few minutes without looking up and thought about what it said:

She was proud of him and loved his letters. He knew that. She wanted him to think she was feeling better, but she wasn't planning to move anytime soon. An indication her health hadn't improved. Then it was her advice to her son. Spend your evenings learning. Be brave. Trust God. Recurring themes to be sure, but they took on a new meaning when she died within six months of writing the letter. She knew he would need another anchor.

He would keep the letter close while he figured things out. He needed direction right now, and for the time being, he was done talking to God. He had always looked to Mother anyway.

His chest was tight. He refolded the letter, exhaled slowly, and put it back in his pocket.

Edward Hambleton completed the sale of Paynefield to Lawrence Andrews for $5,500 in September of 1905.

CHAPTER 3:

Dead Ends

In the fall of 1892, Henry, Frank's oldest brother, developed the "lung trouble" so common at that time and the doctor recommended heading west. Frank eagerly quit his job and went with him. They didn't really have a plan. They were just going west to see what new experience awaited them… and, of course, to work toward improving Henry's health.

They started west through Chicago and stayed just a few days looking through stockyards and attending a celebration for the Grand Army of the Republic. When they got off the train in Las Vegas, they met a Pueblo Native, a small man with a blanket wrapped around him, held in place by a belt. Frank had read *The Last of the Mohicans* and "*The Deerslayer*" by James Fenimore Cooper and was expecting something different. He decided his image of the "noble Redman" might not have been very accurate; but he was excited to meet whatever this new life had waiting for them.

Their first opportunity came when a couple of deer hunters, John Albright and Horace Yeoman, came to town. Frank and Henry were curious about their string of horses carrying deer, about the kind of life they lived, and about the possibility of making a living for themselves by doing what they both enjoyed, hunting. They visited the deer hunters' camp several times over the next few days. Eventually the hunters offered to include them in their group and pay them a set wage every month. The brothers accepted and spent that winter hunting deer in the mountains north of Santa Fe, New Mexico. The air was clean, and Henry's health improved.

In the summer they prospected for gold with the same group of men, but with less luck. The following fall, a rumor spread that there was a lot of gold to be found along the San Juan River. Ready for a change in fortune, they all went to Albuquerque to get outfitted for the promise of finding gold.

Sixty miles outside of Albuquerque, trouble struck. Henry started to cut wood so they could cook dinner. He slipped on the snow and swung the axe deep in his leg. It was a significant wound. But the men were young, and they decided to tough it out.

By the time they reached a trading post in Rock Springs, 40 miles away, Henry's leg was hot and red; and he was in a lot of pain. Albright and Yeoman went on ahead. Disappointed, Frank and Henry had no choice but to stay and concentrate on Henry's leg.

George Bennet and his wife, the owners of the trading post, did their best for Henry. They made sure there was plenty of clean water and towels and helped him move around the room. But the leg got worse. Knowing that Henry needed more help than they could give him, George made the long trip to Albuquerque to get some medicine. He came back with some oil, carbolic acid, and instructions on how to mix them and swab the leg. Even swabbing it every three hours, the wound didn't seem to be getting any better. It quit getting worse, but they needed more than that if they were ever going to be able to move forward. One day, entirely by accident, Frank put the swab in the carbolic acid instead of the diluted mixture. The next morning the infected cells died and fell out, and the leg finally began to heal.

Rumors about the gold along the San Juan River reached the trading post, and George Bennet was itching to try his hand at prospecting. After talking it over, the Noel brothers decided to buy out the trading post instead of chasing after gold. George Bennet left, and they stayed to become store-keepers and Indian traders.

They spent that winter trading with local ranchers and Natives nearby. They collected pelts, jewelry, and lovely hand-made woolen items to sell in Albuquerque. All the while, they were buying things on their good name and dreaming of getting enough profit to set them up financially.

In the spring, they loaded everything in a wagon and rode the 100 miles back into the city, excited about selling everything for a profit and having a nest egg for the future. They were met with heart-wrenching disappoint-ment. Prices had fallen. They were told their goods were not worth very much in the current market. To make matters worse, they had a heavy tab at the store for items they needed during the winter. If they left everything they had, the store owners told them, they would call it even. They could hardly believe what they were hearing. All the work, all the dreaming of a bright future, and they would be left with nothing? Frank and Henry felt they had no choice. Reluctantly, they left everything—every pelt, every piece of jewelry, every hand-woven blanket, and every dollar they had—to pay their debt. For Frank and Henry, it was a shocking dead end.

The next morning, they woke up with no breakfast and no money. There was nothing to trade at their trading post. They had brought it all with them. So trading was over. They had very few prospects, which meant they were open to just about anything. Splitting up was the last thing they wanted to do, but they had to do something.

They heard of a company looking for men to build a road. Frank put on his best suit, went to the boss, and was flatly turned down. Not wanting to give up, he changed into his work clothes, went to the straw boss, and was hired on the spot...with an advance. They had money for a meal and a place to stay for a few days!

Frank did his best on the job. After all, someone was paying him for his work. But there were moments of feeling at loose ends, directionless. Nothing he had tried so far had taken root. He had not become a hunter, a prospector, or an Indian trader. He was nowhere close to building a home of his own. And he didn't see things changing anytime soon. In those moments he would take out his mother's letter again and reread it. *"Remember how young you are and how much you have to learn."* I'm trying, Mother. I'm really trying.

In the meantime, Henry met a Spanish traveling man and they got to talking about the trading business he and Frank had lost. Despite their bad experience in Albuquerque, the three men eventually decided to try trading again. When the last of the money came in from the sale of Paynefield, the three started a store in Naseomento, New Mexico, and immediately saw some success. They were doing so well, in fact, that over time they attracted the attention of a rich Mexican entrepreneur. Before long, their Spanish partner asked them to buy out his share of the store. They weren't sure why he wanted out. Things were going well. But they bought him out and he left.

His reasons soon became clear when their former partner and the Mexican entrepreneur opened up a larger store nearby. Business for the Noel brothers began to shrink noticeably. It felt like a betrayal. But what could they do? As their business continued to shrink, they knew they needed to do something else to bolster their income. But what?

While they were still trying to hang on to the store, word about gold surfaced again. Their clerk, Buck Fronz, and another of their friends, Jack Martin, heard that gold was plentiful in Holbrook, Arizona. The message they received was "Gold! Come quick...!" So the three men—Buck, Jack, and Frank—left Henry to run the store and they headed west.

It was the hardest trip Frank had ever made up to that point. The first night was the worst. They traveled south through Albuquerque to Gallup, where there was already snow and the promise of wind on the mesa. Frank talked about making camp there, but he was a lot younger than the other two men, so his opinion landed on deaf ears. The others thought they should tough it out. They pressed on toward Holbrook.

Four miles up on the mesa, the wind was driving the snow in sheets so dense that they couldn't see the road and the horses couldn't move forward. They turned their covered wagon broadside to the wind, unhooked the horses, and put the horse blankets on them; then they tied the harnesses back on, just to keep the blankets from blowing away. Inside the wagon, they took apart one of the beds and stuffed the blankets and quilts between the canvas and the bows that held the cover up over the wagon. That kept out a bit of the cold. The wind rocked the wagon through the night, only failing to turn it over because of the weight of their camping supplies and horse food. Snow and sleet pelted the wagon and made sleep an impossibility. They lit some candles for light.

Finally, around midnight, the storm started to ease up a bit, and they started to breathe a bit easier.

In the morning, snow and snowdrifts made their progress slow. They fed their horses grain and pushed on until they found a spot with both timber and water. Finally, they were able to make camp, start a fire, and enjoy a good meal and a bit of a rest.

Over the next few days, the cold just followed them. They rode 25 to 30 miles each day, camped where there was adequate timber and water, talked about the gold that was waiting for them in Holbrook, dreamed about what they would do with it, and tried to get warm.

When they finally arrived, they were pleased to see there was no snow. But the good news ended there. The friend who encouraged them to come explained that there was lots of gold, all right, just about anywhere you wanted to pan for it. But when you tried to pick it up, it broke into hundreds of little flakes and floated to the ground. No one had figured out a way to collect it.

Another disappointing dead end.

They stayed with their friend and his family for about a week, trying to decide what to do next. But they soon felt that it was time to contribute to the household or move on.

They heard about a temporary job opportunity to run the mail from Holbrook over the mountain to the people of the Tonto Basin on the other side. Their regular mail carrier had nearly lost his life in the storm Frank's group had come through earlier, The mail had been lost, and he had frozen his feet so badly that he had to quit. People in the Tonto Basin were already getting antsy with no word of the outside world. So, the post-master offered to pay well for anyone who would get the mail through— just one time. After that, it should be warmer and easier to make the trip, and he had people who could do it. There was a cabin on the mountain for the mail carriers, and the path was clearly marked by blazes on the trees in both directions.

The friends talked it over and decided that Buck and Frank would take the job. It didn't bother Frank that he had never run mail before. He was open to anything that promised to add some excitement and income. It was only a temporary job; it would pay well; and it would be a good distraction from his thoughts. How was Henry doing at the store? Would they end up losing this one, too? If so, what was his next step?

They started out.

The first day went well. The weather was clear and warm when they left Holbrook. By the time they got to the cabin further up the mountain, they were in a foot of snow. But the weather was still clear, and the cabin had some provisions for their evening meal. They brought food for the horses with them and had plenty of snow to make water.

The next day was much more difficult. The sky was clear, but the climb was very steep, and the snow kept getting deeper. They took turns leading the way to give the horses and themselves a break. Luckily the good weather held, and they pressed on. When they got to the timber line, they knew they were getting close. At last, they were standing on the rim rock at the top! When they looked down into the valley, they could see people and horses going about their daily lives.

The descent down the mountain was just as steep and required a lot of slow zigzagging to keep from sliding to the bottom. By the time they got halfway down, the townspeople spotted them and began to climb up to meet them. They were so grateful to get their mail, they treated Frank and Buck like heroes. For the next couple of days, they had a place to stay, good food for themselves and their horses, and tours around the valley. No charge. The hospitality had a renewing effect.

When it finally came time to leave, they were fed and rested and optimistic about the future. They headed back to Holbrook by a longer, flatter route, but still made it back in good time. They got paid, settled finances with their host family, and ended their short careers as mail carriers.

A relatively short, but this time profitable, dead end.

The trip back to Naseomento was a painful one for Frank. A couple of days out and they were back in 18 inches of snow. One evening when he was lighting a fire, the sulphur from the match blew back into his eyes and it really stung. Soon after, he developed snow blindness. He didn't see anything for three days. The going was slow. Buck, of course, had to lead the way. And Frank was in excruciating pain day and night. A doctor in a town they were passing through gave him some salve for his eyes, and, while that provided a little relief, he was still in constant pain.

By the time they got back to Naseomento, they were both exhausted, and sick of the snow. In their absence, Henry had taken a horse and wagon in partial trade at the store. That decision benefited them later, but it was not enough to save the store. After a year in the trading business, with sales dwindling, the brothers decided to look for something else. Again, the question was, what?

Nothing seemed to hold their interest. At 21, Frank had lived on a plantation in the East, worked in a bank with his uncle, hunted deer in the West, thought about panning for gold (but didn't), helped build roads, owned and lost two trading posts, and run the mail, but nothing stuck.

Eventually, the Noel brothers ended up in Fruitland, New Mexico. With a wagon and a good team of horses, they established a freight business, running goods from Durango, Colorado, or Gallup, New Mexico, about 150 miles. Edmund joined them there and they spent their spare time with other bachelors from the area or visiting some Mormon families that had settled along the San Juan River.

Horseback riding and playing baseball were favorite pastimes, with baseball very high on the list. Frank played with the Fruitland Nine and made the circuit through Colorado and New Mexico. Fruitland loved to watch him play, and they had good attendance at all of their games. After the games there was always a dance they could enjoy with the local girls. Frank looked forward to the dances almost as much as the games.

They lived for a while in a tent on a piece of land owned by their friend, Cyril Collyer. But when Edmund joined them, the brothers started renting spaces and planning to put down roots.

Friends and traders, *standing, left to right:* Frank L. Noel, Henry R. Noel; *seated:* Edmund Noel, Will Evans, Cyril J. Collyer. Frank L. Noel Collection (P-166), L. Tom Perry Special Collections, Harold B. Lee Library, Brigham Young University, Provo, Utah.

*(Will Evans, pictured here with friend Cyril Collier and the 3 Noel brothers, would go on to write **Along Navajo Trails**, one resource for this book and the source for this picture.)* (5)

Frank went to work for yet another company in Colorado, hauling water. This job, too, only lasted about six months. He headed back home to Fruitland, still looking for something he hadn't quite found.

CHAPTER 4:

Life in Mancos

When the Roberts family left their little two-room house next to Chicken Creek, Clark had saved enough to buy some land and decided to build another home that had two rooms upstairs and two rooms downstairs. But before their new home was completely finished, he decided to build an even bigger home! They had so much room in the big house, compared to where they were living before, they invited friends to visit and neighbors to join them for games and dancing in the evenings. They bought the first organ in town, and with Clark's violin, the music and dancing became a regular event.

The children were enrolled in their first school and walked a mile to get there every day. They were shocked the first time they saw a student being spanked by a teacher. It was the first time they had been around non-Mormon families, and they were not used to seeing that form of discipline.

That wasn't the only surprise. It soon became evident to them they were seen as "different" because of their Mormon heritage. In those days, Mormons were often shunned because of their stand on polygamy, and they often lived on one side of town while non-Mormons occupied the other. Non-Mormon children did not play with the Roberts children at first, and sometimes threw rocks at them. There were even separate areas on the playground. The

Mormon girls had a playhouse under one bush and non-Mormon children played elsewhere. That segregation went on for some time.

Clark and Mary Roberts were very involved with the Mormon church. A new stake (local Mormon church district) was organized in July 1885 by Joseph Smith and a few other men whose families were delighted to be able to have meetings again. They started out meeting in different homes for a while, and eventually joined with Weber, a Mormon settlement about five miles from the Roberts' ranch.

Clark was appointed Sunday school superintendent and taught classes. Mary headed up the Relief Society, taking their wagon to minister to families throughout the area. It took three days to go from one end of the stake to the other. Daughters Hattie, Mae, and Jenny often went with her, listening and learning, tending to the babies, and helping in any way they could.

Over time, the helpfulness of the Relief Society, as well as Clark's willingness to act as doctor, dentist, and veterinarian, gained them respect, and the tension between the two groups began to ease up.

For the most part, these were happy years for the Roberts family, productive years, hopeful years. Evenings were spent as a family, reading, singing, playing games, talking about the day, and evening prayers. There was lots of laughter. Three more babies were born.

The children enjoyed listening to their parents' adventures. Like the time their father had the mail route over Ute Indian country and the Utes went on the warpath. The mail route was long, and Clark had to camp out in the open to complete it. Officials came to take Mary and the children to the stockade for their protection. But Clark believed that, if they showed no fear, and were respectful and kind with the Natives they came in contact with, they should be okay. If they showed fear, it could cost them dearly. So Mary refused to go to the stockade, and they both tried to carry on as if they had no fear. It wasn't easy, but it turned out to be the right thing to do. One morning, when Clark woke up, he saw horse tracks around his camp, but there wasn't a person in sight. The next morning, the same thing happened. But as he started to ride away, he was joined by two Natives, one riding on each side of him. They were there to protect him as he rode through a dangerous area on his trip back home. One of the Natives told Clark he had a brave wife. While he was gone, Natives had been to his home and his wife offered them food and rest. They were not used to being received with such kindness. Word spread that this couple was different. And they would be protected.

The children felt lucky to have such brave parents. They also learned the importance of treating all people with respect. That was a lesson Mae never forgot.

In the fall, the children would gather nuts with two other families who had children about the same ages. The three families would picnic, explore the countryside, enjoy the bright colors of autumn, and play in the leaves as they fell from the trees.

Winters were full of happy, snowy memories. The family rode in a sleigh pulled by their horses. Sleigh bells danced and children laughed and sang. Parents happily joined in, making sure everyone was tucked snugly in enough layers to ward off the cold.

Of course, it wasn't all happiness and light. There were hard times too. Like the time smallpox made its way through the villages around Mancos. It sprang up near Weber, the Mormon community near them. So, instead of quarantining families that had the disease, the authorities simply drew a line just outside of Weber and very near the new Mormon meeting place. No one was to cross that line. Church was canceled until the disease ran its course. The only person in Weber to actually contract the disease was a lady who had been tending others who were sick. She isolated herself, religiously applied olive oil to her skin—a common "remedy" at the time—and recovered.

There was also the time Clark was excommunicated from the Mormon church over some disagreement with his partners in a flour mill. That was one of the hardest times, because his love of God and the church were never in question. Exactly what the disagreement was, or how it was related to his faith, I don't know. He was eventually reinstated.

Similarly, there was the time when one of the ranch hands fell in with some men who convinced him to help them steal some of the Roberts' livestock. They never did recover any of the animals, but the ranch hand came back years later, apologized, and said he had fallen on hard times. Clark forgave him, gave him $5, and told him to go live a good life. Then, Clark humbly and honestly promised he would also try to live a good life.

Over the years, Clark's health was slowly but steadily failing. Rheumatism made it increasingly hard for him to do the physical work he was used to doing. His aching joints caused him to look south for a warmer climate. Their good friends, the Youngs, were going to live in Mexico, so Clark went with them to see if that would be a better climate for his family too.

Clark's absence left their son, Orville, to do most of the chores. Mae and Jenny, now teenagers, helped him as much as they could. Mary managed everything else; but it was a lonely business without Clark.

Just before Christmas, the whole family came down with the flu.

On Christmas Eve, Mary sent Orville to the post office, hoping the family would at least have a letter from Clark telling how he was doing and that he would be home soon. When Orville returned, he was covered in snow and smiling. He had a letter from his father! The whole family sat together to listen while Mary read it, eager to hear the news. When would Daddy be home?

Their hope turned to disappointment when she read that Clark would probably be gone at least another month. Quiet settled around the room.

What they didn't know was that, when Clark approached the Mexican border, he decided to turn back. He reasoned that, if the weather at the border was as warm as it was in the winter, it would be too hot in the summer to get any work done. He actually caught the same train back that his letter did! At the train station, he set out on foot through the snow toward home. Orville, riding in the wagon, completely missed him. When Clark finally got home, he swung open the door and yelled, "Christmas gift!"

Mary immediately fainted. Orville caught her. Hattie took the baby that had been in Mary's lap. And they completely forgot all about being disappointed.

The Railroad

October 24, 1893, was an important day for the Roberts family. Their son Howard married Mary Young and prepared to move to Mexico, where his wife's family lived. On the same day, Orville turned 21 and set out to make a new life of his own. With the two older boys gone, and their father in pain, it left Jenny and Mae, now teenagers, to do most of the work the boys had done. Their brother Frankie was a willing and efficient worker, but, with curvature of the spine, he was limited in some things. He often drove the wagon, negotiated with shopkeepers, and contributed in any way he could. But a lot of the harder labor was left to the older girls. Hattie and Daphne were needed to help take care of the house and the two youngest boys.

When the railroad threatened to cut through his ranch, Clark was in bed and could not get out to negotiate with the railroad officials for his property, as his neighbor, Mr. Bauer, was doing. As it turned out, that didn't matter.

Mr. Wigglesworth, an official at the railroad, had a horse that went lame. When he asked around for a vet, he was referred to Clark Roberts, who tended animals when the need arose. Mr. Wigglesworth sent a hired man to see if Clark could help and was told to bring the horse to his barn. Clark looked over the situation, told his boys what to do, they did it, and the horse recovered. When the hired man came to get the horse, he asked what the charge would be. Clark told him there would be no charge if Mr. Wigglesworth came to get the horse himself. Otherwise, it would cost $100. Clark wanted a meeting with the railroad official.

Curious and eager to save money, Mr. Wigglesworth came to retrieve his horse and find out what Clark wanted. Unable to show him around the ranch, Clark invited him to walk around on his own and look at it with an eye toward making a railroad station there. There was a new barn that could be used for the depot with plenty of room for the tracks to run by. There was a house that the agent could live in. And there were 40 acres that could be turned into anything the railroad needed it to be. The truth was, Clark explained, he was no longer able to work the land; so he could be convinced to sell for the right price.

Mr. Wigglesworth walked the property and began to envision a railroad station. He asked Clark to name his price. There was no negotiation. Within 10 days, without ever leaving his bed, Clark had a check for the full amount he had asked for.

Plus, he got an extra $25 for winning a bet with his neighbor, Mr. Bauer.

CHAPTER 5:

Life in Fruitland

C lark decided their next home would be in New Mexico. The main Mormon settlement there was in Fruitland, a farming community about 15 miles from Farmington on the San Juan River. It was close to a city and sounded promising.

It was an eventful trip.

On their way, they stopped to rest and water their stock at a place called West Water. An old Native there, perhaps tired of white men taking what they wanted, pointed a gun at Clark's head and told him the water belonged to him and he needed it for his goats. Having learned he should show no fear, but remain respectful, Clark pushed the gun to one side and gave the Native some money. He acknowledged the other man's goats needed water, and he asked the old man to water them until they had their fill. Then he would water his stock with what was left over. Evidently the goats had just been watered, because they refused to drink. The Roberts' animals got all the water they needed. The old man scowled. Clark smiled, and the Roberts family went on to find a place to camp out.

When dinner was over, everyone started to settle in for the night. Animals watered, dishes done, bedrolls pulled out, and prayers said, they looked forward to a restful night.

They didn't get it.

About 4 a.m., Clark woke up with a fear he couldn't identify. He checked the camp, and all seemed to be in order. The distant thunder told him it would be raining soon. Then it hit him. They were in a box canyon, a horrible place to be in if there should be a flash flood. "Wake up! Wake up, everybody! We have to move NOW!"

The sleepy family picked up everything and headed toward the mouth of the canyon and higher ground. Almost immediately, they saw water pour over the spot where they had been sleeping minutes before. Clark bowed his head. *Thank you, Lord, for waking me up!*

The next morning, they were grateful to be able to continue on their way.

⸙

Once they arrived in Fruitland, life took on a very different rhythm. They built a home in the city, but, in the fall, they pitched a tent in an orchard in Farmington, about 10 miles away, and picked fruit. Many other families did the same thing. They picked fruit during the day, peeled it and cut it into strips for drying in the evening, and sometimes held dances in the big fruit house. When picking season was over, they returned home with enough fruit and money to see them through the winter.

Another change they dealt with during the summer was the lack of water. Mae and Jenny milked cows, hoed weeds, irrigated and plowed the fields, and did the heavy farm work. During a drought, the family was forced to haul water from the creek to the fruit trees and garden. It was back-breaking, time-consuming work. Many families gave up and left. Clark tried to build a reservoir to store water and they stayed. But the effort to build the reservoir took its toll. Clark, in pain most of the time now, found it even harder to keep up. They started selling off their livestock to make ends meet.

Eventually, Mary took Mae and Jenny and found work packing and drying fruit in Farmington. In the beginning, the younger children stayed home with Clark. Daphne, the third oldest girl, did her best to keep the house running, but she was only 12. When her mother and sisters came home on the weekends, they would try to do as much as they could to get the family ready for the following week.

It was a valiant effort but, eventually, Mary decided it was too much. She needed to be home, and the family needed to be together. They moved into a big tent set up in a peach orchard, where they could work together, drying fruit. It was rustic living to say the least. But they knew how to do rustic, and the family was happy to be together again, for as long as their situation would allow. Jenny played the harmonica, Mae capered around dancing, and their parents laughed until they cried. Clark kept the youngest children in the tent with him while the older children and Mary worked the fruit. They started dreaming of the day they would all be together in a spacious home again all year long.

Having the family all together was wonderful, but it eventually began to bother Mary that there was no school for the children in Jackson. Education had been important to her mother, and it was important to her. It was time for another change. She gathered the children and found a house to rent in Mancos, about 50 miles north. She found a job while the children were in school and went home when she could to check on Clark, who moved back into the house in Fruitland.

The infrequent visits were hard on everyone. Mary and the girls worried about how Clark was doing without help. Clark wandered around a house that had suddenly become very quiet.

Luckily, they had built their home near a main road. Their well near the road was an invitation for travelers to stop, water their horses and chat a while. Clark really looked forward to the company and would not fail to tell people about God's goodness if they would listen.

The older girls found entertainment by having house parties, playing baseball, and going to dances. Often it meant going 14 miles in the wagon, but by this time, they had been handling their team of horses for years. They enjoyed the dances, so the distance was not an obstacle.

On Sundays, they would walk a mile to church. In the winter, when the snow was deep, they remembered gliding over the very same wintery roads in their horse-drawn sleigh when Clark was more able to work. Now they were trudging through wet snow with their feet and hands bitterly cold. Their circumstances had certainly changed.

In the spring, they moved back to Fruitland and rented a small place, taking care of bees for the neighbors. Howard, their older brother, was back from Mexico, and, in his big-brother way, warned the girls that he heard that some non-Mormon boys had moved into the area. The girls were to guard themselves against falling for any of them, he cautioned. It would be best if they stuck with their own kind.

CHAPTER 6:

Turning Point

The very next day after Howard's warning, Edmund and Frank Noel, who were renting the property right next to the Roberts, came out to irrigate their field. Jennie and Mae, ignoring the warning from their older brother, made a bet as to who could get Frank's attention first. The next time the Noel brothers came out to irrigate, the girls were watching from a window with glee as Frank's little pony dumped him in the middle of a ditch. He must have cut quite a figure sprawled in that ditch because, after that, Mae made it a point to be out working in the garden or completing some other outside chore when he came by. On those days, she tried to look her best.

Frank noticed.

They found they had a lot in common. They both played baseball. They both loved going to dances. They both loved their families, and the idea of family. There were differences, of course. Their upbringings were **very** different. Frank and his brothers had been raised on Paynefield, a prosperous plantation in the east, as had their father and grandfather. Mae was not quite four when her family set out on a wagon train. When they settled in Mancos, it was in a two-room house with lots of siblings. Frank's parents were both dead. Mae's parents were still very much alive, and very involved in her life. Both sets of parents loved and trusted God. But Frank's family was skeptical of Mormonism. Mae's family and life were not only bathed in the Mormon teachings, but her parents were on a first-name basis with Joseph Smith and Brigham Young. Still, it wasn't long before Frank and Mae were horseback riding together, going to games and dances, and looking forward to seeing each other when they could.

At the same time, Frank had grown tired of drifting from one thing to the next. He decided it was time to get serious about building a career that would last, and a home and family he could be proud of.

He met a man named Joe Wilkins, who had traded with the Navajo people before, as Frank and Henry had done. The three men decided to go into business together. They got an expensive government license to operate on the Navajo reservation and started a trading post next to an arroyo. It was about 75 miles north of Gallup and 50 miles southwest of Fruitland, and they called it Two Grey Hills. To begin with, it was just a big tent with the supplies they brought in on two wagons. But they got busy building. Henry and Joe and a Navajo helper began making adobe bricks, 12" x 8". Frank got busy hauling what they needed the 75 miles from Gallup. He brought in wood, building supplies, and goods to sell. In time they had a two-room building, and were able to move in just before the cold weather set in. The large room was for the store and the smaller room was their living quarters: bedroom, kitchen, and living room all in one. Their beds were the bedrolls they tossed down at the end of a long day.

It was a start. Frank was 23 and beginning to dream about building a future. It would not be easy.

Sometimes, Two Grey Hills felt like 100 miles from nowhere. It was a two-to-three-day drive one way in the wagon to get supplies. Allowing time to rest the horses, each round trip took the better part of a week. When he got back to the trading post, there wasn't a lot to divert his attention. The routine was: get up, work the store with Henry and Joe, get ready for the next day, go to bed, repeat. Even the scenery around him was monotonous.

They were surrounded by dusty hill after dusty hill. The only real color was in an endless sky at sunrise and sunset. In those moments the sky was truly inspiring, a welcome respite from the dust, and a reminder of something or Someone much larger than man.

Weeks turned into months.

When the isolation got too bad, Frank would make the two-day trip to Fruitland to see Mae. Her parents, however, made it clear that they did not want her to marry a non-Mormon boy. And while he was sure she delighted in his company, as he did in hers, he was also sure that she loved her parents and did not want to disappoint them. Frank's brother, Henry, wasn't too keen on the idea of him dating a Mormon girl either. Their visits were sporadic, and they were hearing caution from both sides.

Frank began to build a log cabin near the adobe building that held the store. He added mud plaster between the logs and mud over the roof logs to make it cool in the summer and warm in the winter.

Mae's watchful parents decided it was a good time to send her off to Brigham Young Academy in Provo, Utah. This served two purposes. The first was to continue Mae's education. Brigham Young had officiated at her parents' wedding, and they trusted him completely. The second, of course, was to get her away from Frank, who, from their perspective, was becoming more and more of a concern,

Frank was not easily deterred. He went to visit Mae in Provo around Christmas and they had a great time. They went horseback riding and decided to ask Mae's sister, Jennie, to go with them on a train ride to a dance in Mona. A chaperone meant they could go without a scandal.

As it turned out, Mae's mother was also in Provo at the time. And while she appreciated the fact that they had a chaperone for their trip, she was increasingly afraid that Frank was becoming too important to Mae. It was time to put a stop to it. When it was time for Frank to go home, she demanded they stop seeing each other completely and for good.

On the one hand, the thought of not seeing each other was unimaginable. On the other hand, they had both been taught to respect their parents. Mae's parents were loving and only wanted what they believed was best for her. They both knew that. Frank only wished he could still turn to his own parents. What would they advise? He would never know.

It hurt, but the young couple decided to honor Mae's parents. They would do their best and move on. They would force themselves to focus on other things. Frank quietly made the trip back to the routine of Two Grey Hills.

Still in Provo, Mae decided to start a kindergarten with her sister, Jennie. It would keep her busy and it would be something good for the community. Maybe she would be so busy she wouldn't think about Frank that much. Maybe. They borrowed chairs, put up notices, and made a start. She would take one day at a time. Life would certainly go on.

Wouldn't it?

On the third day of the second week, Jennie broke out with measles. Three days later, Mae had the spots too. Classes were canceled. They would just have to wait to reopen the school when they were healthy.

They never did.

A letter to the editor of the **Deseret Evening News** published June 27, 1897, reads as follows:

Fruitland, New Mexico, 17 June 1897

A sad misfortune befell us on the afternoon of Tuesday, the 14th.

Recently, the A.P.R.R. [railroad] donated an iron bridge to span the San Juan River with the understanding that it should be erected on the most direct feasible route leading from Farmington to Gallup, New Mexico.

Messrs. Coe, King, and Phelps had been appointed to a committee to investigate and report. They reached here [Fruitland] Tuesday noon and requested to be put across the river. The boat is a small one and has to be rowed. The carriage was taken apart and placed on the boat and H.D. [Howard] Roberts, Cyril Collyer, Henry R. Noel, and Mr. King started over with the first load.

A light wind was blowing down the river; the wind and the strong current swept the boat downstream under the high perpendicular wall on the west side of the river. The men, fearing the boat would go under leaped out and swam for the eastern shore.

Messrs. Collyer and Noel made the shore without much difficulty. Mr. King was carried down a half mile, reached shore, and ran and caught the boat which had carried its load safely past the rapids – but Mr. Roberts was drowned.

Mr. Roberts was the son of O.C. [Clark] and Mary Coray Roberts, and as L.D. S., had passed through the temple and was embued with the spirit of the gospel. He leaves a wife in a delicate condition and three small children; also, his parents who are breaking with age and hard work and a large circle of relatives who deeply mourn his loss. (3)

The sisters were stunned. Their brother, Howard, was dead, drowned in the San Juan River. A letter from their mother told them she desperately needed them to come home. So they closed the school, returned the chairs, and hurried home.

Back in Fruitland, they found their mother heartsick. Grief over the loss of her son, and concern for his wife and children, consumed all of her thoughts. Not much else mattered. One day at a time, the women held each other up and started to try to make sense of Howard's death. They already missed him so much. Their only solace was the promise they would see him again in the afterlife.

Then, one day, Mae ran into Frank on the road. They had a lot to talk about. Howard's death. Frank's brother, Henry, being there with Howard at the time. It could have been both of them! They talked of family and of loss. Their hearts were broken… but knitted even closer together.

They realized that staying apart was not working for either of them. Their roots were separate, but securely entwined… and that would always be true.

People on both sides continued to give opinions about the perils of a "mixed marriage." Mary, watching them together, decided it was time for Mae to return to school.

This time, it was Frank who loaned her the money. He truly loved Mae and wanted only the best for her. The best, he thought, would be to know her heart away from all of the family opinions. Maybe her leaving for school would be a good thing for them. Maybe he would lose her forever. It was time to find out.

Mae prayed for guidance. She had been praying about Frank since they met two years earlier. Sometimes she just prayed that God would give her what and who she wanted. Sometimes she really wanted God to show her His plan for her. She decided to ask for guidance and went to the home of

President Woodruff of the Mormon church. She explained her dilemma. There was Frank, whom she didn't want to live without. But he was not Mormon. There was another young man, a Mormon, who was interested in her. Was that the way she should go?

President Woodruff looked her in the eyes and said, "Sister, forget the Mormon boy. You only love one boy. Go home and tell him to be baptized. Then marry him."

It seemed so surprisingly simple! But would Frank agree? She would contact him immediately.

When he heard of it, he wrote, "You did right in going to see the president, and when I go into Fruitland, I will be baptized, and when you meet your boy you will meet him as a Latter-Day-Saint." There would be no problem.

Except, it didn't work out exactly that way.

Frank did go into Fruitland and ask for baptism. He was advised to wait until he knew more about the faith. Disappointed, he went back to Two Grey Hills, where his brothers made fun of him for saying he would join the Mormon church just to please Mae and her parents.

Wasn't the God their parents had worshipped the same God? Why did he need to join another church? That kind of decision never works. What does "unequally yoked" mean anyway? Is denomination really that important? Was it the idea of polygamy that he liked? Was he, maybe, looking to eventually marry more than one wife? The teasing went on.

Frank ignored them and assured Mae they could go ahead with their plans. He needed time to know more about the Mormon church, or the church wouldn't baptize him. He was willing. He planned to be baptized within a year.

It never happened.

Mae was always disappointed by that. She loved her church and believed in its teachings. But she expresses her powerful feelings about Frank in this excerpt from a poem she wrote to him. Date unknown. There is more, but you will get the idea.

I Kissed You (excerpt Book of Remembrance) (6)

You kissed me. My heart
My breath, my will
In delicious joy
For a moment stood still.

Life had for me then
No temptations, no charms
No visions of happiness
Outside of your arms.

And were I this instant
An angel possessed
Of the peace and the joy
That are given the blest,

I would fling my white robes
Unrepiningly down.
I would tear from my forehead
Its beautiful crown.

To nestle once more
In that haven of rest
Your lips upon mine
My head on your breast.

They were married October 3, 1898, in Jackson, New Mexico.

CHAPTER 7:

The Wedding

To say the wedding was small is a huge understatement. It was miniscule. They were in an old adobe building that had two rooms. A table was set the full length of the larger room, with a white tablecloth. Quilts were used as cushions on the benches. The table was loaded with food that Mae's mother and sisters, Jennie and Hattie, had prepared.

Frank and Mae sat in two chairs in the middle of the room while family and friends stood along the walls. Even though they had opposed the match, Mae's family loved her, and they filled the room. Frank's brother Edmund was there, but Henry stayed at the store. Mae wore a white dress of Irish lace and a blue ribbon in the ringlets of her hair. Frank wore a dark suit with a starched white collar. That starchy collar, in itself, was proof beyond any doubt that this was indeed a special occasion.

Mae's parents sat near the couple, as did Bishop Ashcroft, who performed the short ceremony.

After the vows were exchanged, everyone surrounded the table where the modest feast was waiting. Mae's father, Clark, asked the blessing, and everyone began to relax and share their stories, happy for the rare opportunity to reconnect. Who knew how long it would be before they were all together like this again?

After dinner, Frank had arranged a dance in Fruitland, 15 miles away. Those who were not going to the dance began to say their good-byes. It was a bittersweet time for all of them. One chapter was closing forever. Another was opening. No one could know how that next chapter would read. They only knew they were moving forward, and the young couple would be miles away in the middle of the desert.

As soon as they could, the couple headed toward the dance.

The dance started at 8 p.m. and they danced until midnight. At midnight everyone took a break to have another big dinner. Then they danced again until 4 a.m.

Finally, it was time to head home. The couple left the dance, escorted by Jennie and a friend named Burt. They drove the wagon across the San Juan River and began the 50-mile trek to Two Grey Hills. That river became a symbol of the change in their lives. One side held the old life they had known before. The other side opened up to a life they had never known. The life they were to share as husband and wife.

Their first nights were spent under the stars, camping in the desert between Fruitland and Gallup. Their first breakfasts were cooked over a campfire. And they were content to have it just that way. They both loved camping and the outdoors. They both loved looking at the stars at night. They both wondered what the future would be like, glad they would find out together.

When they arrived at Two Grey Hills, Frank's brother Henry and a friend were there to greet them. There wasn't another woman for miles. The couple headed for the little log cabin.

Mae looked around her new home, the one Frank had built with his own hands. They were missing a few things that most young brides take for granted. There were no curtains on the windows, no walls to add privacy to their bedroom, no decorations, and no running water.

They did have the camping dishes they had brought with them, four chairs, a rocker, a small cookstove, a small table and dresser, and a bed with no springs. The cupboards were made from old supply boxes stacked on top of each other. Pieces of cardboard were cut to fit for shelves. Water was to be carried from the spring about 150 yards from the house. Firewood would have to be cut regularly for cooking and warmth. It was actually just a little more than they had camping under the stars.

But they were together, and it was enough.

CHAPTER 8:

Two Grey Hills

The days soon fell into a predictable routine. Frank woke up and went to the store while Mae started breakfast. After breakfast, she began transforming their one room into a home with curtains, a little paint, and a few flowers. When she could, she helped Frank in the store and continued the transformation there. The floors were swept and the shelves dusted regularly. She added curtains and a bit of paint, and Two Grey Hills began to look very respectable. She learned how to make the sales, stock the shelves, and greet their Navajo customers, even before she began to learn their language.

The stocked shelves of the store were behind fencing that was easy to see through. This area, in the middle of the room, was called the bullpen. Customers would stand in the bullpen, point to what they wanted, and someone would fetch it for them and put it on the counter. Once a sale was complete with cash or trade, the next person in line would start to point at what they needed. This provided good one-on-one attention to the customers, and it didn't take them long to approve of Mae as the new store helper.

Frank, Henry, and Joe were also busy working with customers, planning what they needed on their next supply run, and trying their best to keep water fetched and firewood chopped for both the house and the store.

As they settled into a routine, the newlyweds started learning a few things about married life. For example, Mae learned that it was best to make requests of Frank *after* a good meal and not while he was tired and hungry. She also learned that it was easier to get things done if she could make Frank think it was his idea. (This is an idea she passed along to my mother with less success.)

Frank learned to take his hat off and clean his boots before coming into the house. He learned Mae liked to know when he was thinking about her. So he should tell her if he thought she looked pretty, or if he wanted to take her to town, or if he just wanted extra time with her.

Frank never really had an opportunity to watch his parents navigate married life. As long as he could remember, his father had been behind closed doors. But Mae's parents had spent decades demonstrating that married life was easier if issues were discussed calmly and openly with both parties having an equal say. Frank and Mae adopted this practice early on and it was to save them a lot of heartache. They also developed a life-long habit of taking a walk in the desert if they had something important to discuss or decide. Not only did they love those walks, but it was easier to think clearly in the outdoors where neither one felt boxed in, there were no distractions, and no one else was around to hear what they needed to say.

Near the end of their first month together, it was time for Frank to go on a supply run to Gallup, and he asked Mae to go with him. She was delighted to have him all to herself, away from the other men and the store. But it turned out to be an extremely uncomfortable trip. That winter was especially hard. The snow was deep and many of the Navajo livestock froze to death in the fields. Another trader, Will Evans, relates seeing a goat who taught itself to walk on its two front legs because the back legs froze and had to be amputated. (5, pg.76) Needless to say, they were both glad to see their warm home again.

As the months went by, the seasonal routine at Two Grey Hills also began to create its own rhythm. In the warm weather, their Navajo customers would come with livestock, or handmade blankets, or jewelry to trade for goods. If they brought a blanket, it would be unrolled on the counter, examined, and a price offered by putting money next to the blanket. If the blanket owner liked the price, he would take the money. If not, he would take the blanket back. Sometimes, the whole transaction would happen without a word being spoken. Good saddle blankets normally sold for between $2.50 and $4. Larger, more ornate rugs would go for $5 to $25.

(Today they are going for hundreds if not thousands. See Chapter 28, "Then and Now," Two Grey Hills.)

Once a year, the government inspector would come by to be sure all was still in good order. These visits were usually uneventful, but welcome opportunities to talk with someone from town.

In the winter, or during hard times, the trading post acted more like a pawn shop. Jewelry, beads, belts, and silver bridles would be left, and both the trader and the customer would take a receipt for the item. When the weather improved, more blankets were made, and the customer would come with things to trade and redeem his property.

In the summer, some of their Navajo friends would help out by making the freight runs for the store. It was a good way for them to earn a little extra money and Frank to have more time at home.

The Noels were intentional in learning about their new Navajo friends and started going to Navajo horse races and celebrations. At one point, Frank decided to enter Mae's little horse, Flaxie, in one of the races. He was so confident that he told Mae she could get a new dress with the money he would win. His confidence was shattered when little Flaxie was left so far in the dust that Frank pulled her out of the race and took her back to Mae with his apologies.

In addition to the Navajos, there were two ladies who lived in a little log cabin several miles from the trading post. Mrs. Cole and Mrs. Eldridge were missionaries among the Navajo people and were widely known and widely respected by both white settlers and Natives. Mae enjoyed visiting them. Mrs. Cole was almost like a mother to her, and Mae felt she could talk to her about things that Frank could only try to understand.

Their isolation in the desert left few options for anything other than their daily routines. Visiting the Navajos and the missionaries, walks in the desert, horseshoes, and horseback riding were the only recreations available to them. So, when they heard there was to be a big dance in Fruitland, the young couple couldn't wait to go.

It would be their first trip back since they were married. Not only would they be able to see their old friends, but they would also be able to share the good news, with some, that they were expecting a baby!

At the dance, they delighted in the laughter of old friends, the opportunity to sway with the music they had been missing since the wedding, and the chance to dance until the sweat ran down their faces. They welcomed the respite from the quiet, dusty hills and tried to find out when the next dance would be.

But their joy was short-lived.

That was the night their first child miscarried.

CHAPTER 9:

Prayer and Hard Work

The miscarriage was devastating. Both Mae and Frank had wanted this baby. Both dreamed of a family that included children. But that dream was not to play out just yet. For Mae, in a culture where getting married and raising children was one of the highest standards for women, it was a heart-wrenching blow. She grieved their loss and worried about the future. Would she ever be able to carry a baby to term? Would she ever be able to realize her dream of being a mother?

Mae went to stay with her mother to recover for a while and Frank went back to the store. But it wasn't long before he came to take his bride home again. For her part, Mae was surprised to realize how happy she was to be going home with him. There wasn't much for her at Two Grey Hills except Frank, and that, she realized, whether children were in her future or not, was enough.

Unfortunately, she was soon sick again, and her mother, Mary, made the trip to Two Grey Hills to take care of her. But Mae was in so much pain this time, they quickly decided it would be better if she were in town where a doctor could treat her. To keep her lying down, they strapped a cot to the back of a wagon. As they slowly traveled the 50 miles back to town, the cot rolled from side to side in the wagon, jarring her swollen joints and causing significant pain. When they finally arrived, Mae had developed a rash of some kind. Bad timing. German measles was working its way through northern New Mexico, so it proved futile to ask anyone to take her in. Frank tried everything he could think of to find someone to help her but had no luck. Mae was in so much pain, she thought she might die, so she asked her mother to pray for her. Mary placed her hands on Mae's head and prayed, and Mae was finally able to drift off to sleep.

My Mother's Hand *by Mary Eliza Roberts Noel (excerpt)*

Is there anything as lovely
Is there anything as grand
Is there anything as tender
As the memory of my mother's hand?

Oh, the blessings that she gave me
With her hand upon my head:
That has thrilled my very being.
It seemed my soul has fled

To a higher place than this one,
To a grander, nobler sphere,
Where pain and suffering leave you
And danger you never fear. (4)

Mae doesn't say what the nature of her condition was. We do know that it was serious enough to move her from Fruitland to a hotel in Durango, Colorado, where there was better medical care. She was told she needed an operation, but she wasn't strong enough to undergo that much stress. She needed to get stronger before they could operate. Only then could she hope to return home.

Frank had to be at the store, so he made the hard decision to leave Mae in Durango with her younger sister Daphne, who came to stay with her until Mae was well. Neither of them had an idea it would take so long.

After about *two months* of resting and trying to get well, there was a conference of Mormon missionaries at the same hotel where the sisters were staying. Mae asked Daphne to go and ask if someone from the conference would come and minister to her. Elder Ensign came.

Mae should tell this in her own words:

> *He, with one of the Elders, came to my room. After giving me a blessing, he told me that the next day, Sunday, they were all going to fast, and if we would join them in the fast, they would all remember me and after meeting they would pray for me. We gladly fasted and prayed for God to bless me and grant that I could get well and in time have the children that I so desired. We went to the meeting, and afterward the Elders joined in a prayer circle for me, and I was administered to. I was thrilled with the power of the Holy Ghost. I have never forgotten that blessing. I knew that God had heard that prayer, and that someday my desire would be granted. I knew that I was better.* (4)

Mae went to the doctor the very next day and he cleared her to have the surgery she had been wanting for so long. He called the hospital and asked them to prepare a room, and she was operated on the following day. Elder Ensign and another elder came and prayed with her before the surgery. He prayed that she would regain her health and that her greatest desire would be honored, to be a mother. She went into the operation with joy, knowing that, after months of trying to get well on her own, God had healed her.

As soon as he could, Frank came to take her from the hospital, but he wanted her to get stronger before making the long journey back home. So he got a room at a hotel, where they stayed for a few more weeks.

While there, they received a telegram that Frank's brother Hambleton was coming to stay. He had developed tuberculosis, as both of his parents had, and was not expected to live much longer. He hoped the clean air and being with family would help. The telegram gave the day and time the train should arrive, so Frank set off to greet his brother. He met the train but couldn't find Hambleton anywhere. Disappointed, he finally walked back to the hotel and found Mae talking with a very sickly stranger who turned out to be his brother. The disease had changed Hambleton so much that Frank didn't even recognize him! He told Mae that night that he was afraid Hambleton would not live long. Nevertheless, as soon as they could, the three set out to make the 100-mile journey, in a wagon, to Two Grey Hills.

The trip was hard on both Mae and Hambleton, so they stopped at her mother's house until they were able to go the rest of the way, and Frank went on ahead. When they were well enough, Mae's brothers, Frank and Don Roberts, set out to escort them to Two Grey Hills.

The San Juan River was running high that spring. The water came all the way up to the sides of the wagon box. The crossing was slow, as the horses strained to pull the wagon through the current. It proved to be a scary crossing, but they were both hopeful and determined. Thankfully, they made it across and reached Two Grey Hills later that night. It was the first time Mae had been home in months, and she was excited to be, once again, by her husband's side in their home.

That winter was hard. Frank was gone a lot, making freight runs for the store in the freezing cold.

Hambleton was still very weak and had to make regular trips to the doctor, 50 miles away. He began a regular routine of exercises and walking in the open air. Eventually he could play horseshoes, and finally was strong enough to ride a horse.

Mae was recovering well but had to spend a lot of time helping Henry in the trading post. Keeping things up there, cooking meals, washing clothes by hand, and hauling water were wearing her down.

The stress of just keeping everything running smoothly started taking a toll on everyone. It was one of those times when little comments or disappointments turn into bigger issues because everyone is so worn out. Henry and Frank found they had different ideas about how the store should run. Energy and patience were at a breaking point.

So, when Mae realized she was expecting another baby, they knew something had to change.

CHAPTER 10:

Motherhood, Camping, and a New House

Frank and Mae owned 40 acres of land in Kirtland, New Mexico, with a small, three-room adobe house on it. They decided to go there, closer to medical attention for both Mae and Hambleton. They believed things would get better there.

That summer *wasn't* much better, though. Hambleton continued to improve little by little, but it was slow. Mae was now in bed most of the time, trying everything she could think of to hold on to this baby. She had a friend, Lucy Burnham, who came and stayed with her, helping her walk from the bed to a nearby chair. So she wasn't able to contribute much. Around that time, Edmund broke his foot and moved in with his brothers to recover. Frank was still running freight for Henry in the store and was able to be home a bit more often. When he was home, he tried a little farming on their property, but mainly had to concentrate on taking care of his wife and brothers.

There was a lot of "recovering" going on at the Noel place. Frank carried a big load and he felt it.

Slowly, though, Mae got stronger and, somewhere around her fourth month, was able to take on her normal chores. Things were slowly improving.

Answered Prayer

On September 11, 1900, their first daughter was born. They named her Clara, after Frank's mother, and she immediately brought into the house a joy they had been missing. When Mary laid Clara in Mae's arms, she told her that she would now get well, and that Clara would be a comfort to her all the days of her life. It was prophetic.

While Clara was still a baby, Frank sold his share of the trading post to Hambleton, but continued to run freight for his brothers occasionally, while he looked for steady work. Sometimes, while he was gone, other bachelor friends would come to visit. Some of them fell into the habit of mockingly asking each other to say grace for the meals that Mae was preparing for them. To Mae, though, the mocking wasn't funny. She resolutely bowed her head, prayed out loud, and let them know that, in her house, they would be grateful for the things God had given them. That's all that was needed. From that time on, grace before a meal was expected and respected.

The following summer, when Clara was about eight months old, Frank took a job with a railroad camp near Durango, Colorado. As soon as he was offered the job, he rode home and asked Mae to join him there, which she gladly did. They brought their cow; bought a tent, a washboard, a few tin dishes, and a tub; and set up housekeeping—or should I say tentkeeping— with their baby. They camped near a stream and enjoyed being by themselves, a family of three, for the first time since they were married.

Days soon fell into a rhythm in the camp too. They got up early, since Frank was working 10-hour days. Mae prepared breakfast and, when Frank left for work, she tended to the baby, milked their cow, and tried to make their tent as appealing as possible. When Frank came home at night, she tried to meet him with a clean baby and a hot supper. He would milk the cow again, make sure there was water and firewood for the next day, and they would talk under the stars before slipping in for the night. They were making money, too. Between Frank's hard work and the team of horses they brought with them to pull heavy loads, they earned as much as $5 a day! (That is the equivalent of $185 in 2023.) It wasn't long before Frank got promoted and earned even more.

An old school friend, Edna Towner, and her husband lived upstream a little. Every few days, they came to the railroad camp to sell meat. Then Edna's husband would go on to town, and Edna and her little son would stay with Mae. They both looked forward to those days.

Sundays were days off, and they would spend them exploring the hills around them and enjoying the good weather. Life was good again.

When little Clara started teething, it was another woman from the camp, a black woman, who coached Mae through it. She came every day, soothed Mae's fears, helped prepare Clara's food, and became a real friend. She was, in a very real sense, a godsend.

When Mae told Frank about it, he was pleased that she had support, but cautioned her not to invite her new friend to eat with them. Mae was surprised by her husband's reaction because she had seen Frank eat with Navajos many times. She realized that, in this way at least, her husband was not as far removed from plantation life as she hoped he was. But she had been taught to honor her husband's requests, so an invitation to the new friend never went out. I would like to have known her name.

By the time Clara began taking her first steps, the cold weather was setting in, and it was time to pack up their tent and move back to the adobe house, where the walls provided good insulation and warmth.

They stayed in the house another year or so, with Frank running freight off and on.

In the spring of 1902, they sold that house and bought another one in Jackson, about 15 miles away. Edmund was still recuperating from his broken foot, so he moved with them. The new house was across the street from Mae's parents, which made it easy for them to visit and support each other.

As the days unfolded, little Clara was learning to talk, much to the delight of everyone who saw her. And…Mae was soon expecting another baby! So, it was a delight for both mother and daughter to be close to each other again.

Frank says he never moved into this house. We can only wonder why. But he stayed for a while in a house owned by a friend. He took a job about five miles away, along the La Plata River, and continued to stay involved in the lives of his wife and daughter.

The new house, where Mae and Clara were, was not adobe, and the weather was hot. So, Frank tried his best to insulate it by hauling green cottonwood saplings, 15 feet long, and putting them against the house for shade. He put in a small crop, and everyone awaited the arrival of the new baby.

CHAPTER 11:

Logs, Dogs, and Two Babies

Jennie Noel was born on June 16, 1902, and was named after Mae's sister, who had been almost like a twin to her. All went well with the delivery, and Jennie was raised knowing she was named after someone her mother couldn't imagine life without.

When Jennie was six weeks old, the little family packed up again. With Mae's brother Don, they went to the mountains, where the weather was cooler, and the men found work as loggers.

The first night there was memorable. It was late and it was cold. Don and Frank started to set up the tents while Mae took the babies to the main house, where meals were being served to the workers. They were tired and cold, and Jennie was crying. Mae tried to soothe her for quite a while with no success. Eventually, the cook asked if she could try something. She took Jennie from her mother, unwrapped her and held her closer to the oven while she rubbed circulation back into her tiny frame. That did the trick. The gracious cook gave Mae some warm catnip tea, and they all began to warm up and relax.

When Frank came to tell them that the tent was up and a fire started, they gladly went with him. After the babies were fed and in bed, they were all able to sleep soundly that night. Don was in his tent. Frank and Mae and the two babies were in theirs. Their tent was small, but they had a cookstove, a bed, a table, and two chairs. And they were together again. They loved the mountain scenery, so different from the dry desert at Two Grey Hills. They went to sleep, that first night, with a smile.

The Logging Camp

Logging is dangerous work. The trees were huge, big enough around that only one tree at a time would fit on the wagon. If a log started to roll while they were trying to load it, they needed to be quick, It was either get out of the way or be crushed. The steeper the mountain patch they were working on, the harder it was to keep a solid footing, and the greater the danger of rolling logs and stumbling over stumps and debris. The men laughingly took it in stride. Mae prayed for them daily.

There was another group of ladies who had come with their children, and they soon became friends. Little Jennie had some problems with colic, and Mae continued to wish she knew more about formula and keeping colicky babies happy. But with other mothers to talk to, the days began to move by swiftly.

One day, Mae went to get water, and when she came back there was a very large dog lying on the floor of the tent, and Clara was sitting right next to him with her little toddler arms around his neck. This was frightening at first, but it soon became clear that the dog was safe and was as fond of Clara as she was of him. It turned out that he belonged to a bachelor who lived up in the mountains. When the man came down for lumber, the dog came with him, but never went back. The man soon realized his dog preferred little Clara's company over his own. Eventually, when the Noels left the mountain, the dog followed them home.

Another day, when the rain was coming down and the wind was blowing, the quilt Mae was trying to hang over the door of the tent came down. Mae exclaimed, "Oh darn it!" At the same time, Clara was stacking bars of soap on a chair, and they came tumbling down too. So she too exclaimed, "Oh darn it!" Mae was startled but knew immediately where those words came from. That's the day she learned not to use words you don't want to hear coming out of the mouths of your children!

Mae dearly loved the flowers that grew around her tent, the clean mountain air, and the unhurried life that camping offered. It must have reminded her of her time as a child in the two-room cabin on Chicken Creek. But when the snow began to fall, they packed up their mountain retreat and prepared to head back down the mountain to a home with thick adobe walls.

Mae never forgot that first night on the road.

A boy they knew had promised to go with them and herd their two cows. They watched for him as they packed, but he never showed up. So the question became, what should they do now? They had planned for him to ride one of the horses and herd the cows while Frank drove the wagon team and Mae tended the babies. They decided they would have to do it all themselves.

Frank tied the extra horse to the back of the wagon. They secured Jennie in a baby buggy behind the seat of the wagon. Clara, now two, was strapped to Mae so she would not roll out of the wagon as it jostled down the trail. That freed Mae's hands to drive the wagon team while Frank rode the other horse and herded the cows in front of the wagon. They hoped to reach Durango by nightfall.

The day started out fine. The weather was cloudy but pleasant. They made a short stop for lunch to give everyone a little break. I don't even want to think of what it was like to strap a two-year-old back to her mother after a bit of freedom! Hopefully, it was naptime.

By the time they reached Durango, it was late, they were tired, and the cows refused to move into town. They stood on the railroad track and didn't budge. The railroad frightened the horse that was tied on the back, so it ran up one side of the wagon and then the other, jerking the wagon both ways. A tired horsewoman, a toddler, and an infant in a strapped-on buggy were thrown from side to side. Frank's voice could be heard close and calm. *"It isn't much farther. Don't lose your nerve."*

Eventually they did make it into town and a hotel. But there were no fires blazing, and Jennie was screaming with cold again. The landlady invited them into the kitchen, where they could warm up, and Jennie finally fell asleep about 10 that night.

There was one more day on the road, then home.

Home.

It was such a welcome sight, with its large fireplace and room to run around. They spent a quiet winter there with Mae's parents, their only neighbors.

Early in 1903 they rented a farm on the La Plata River and moved there. That year, Frank put in crops of hay, wheat, corn, fruits, and vegetables. Mae tried her hand at raising chickens. She got two Plymouth Rock hens and two roosters. Once a week, Frank took the eggs into Farmington, 12 miles away, to sell and buy supplies. They charged 25 cents a dozen and thought they were getting a very good deal. They were up early every day and worked hard. They had everything they needed at the new house but were alone most of the time. At haying time, Frank's brother Henry, and Mae's brothers, Don and Lou, along with some hired hands, helped bring in the hay. At the same time, Mae hired someone to help around the house and prepare for another new baby. The children were growing strong, and Frank and Mae once again began to dream of what their future could look like with enough money and several children around the house.

On January 19, 1904, Frank Leland Noel was born, the image and namesake of his father. Life was very good.

With the addition of their third child, they decided it was time to buy a home of their own.

A Mormon friend of theirs, Luther Burnham, had a place in Fruitland that he wanted to sell. Since they would be closer to friends and the Mormon community, it seemed like a good idea. The farm itself had a nice orchard and there was room to plant crops and a nice garden. It made sense. They moved in around the first of March and began planting crops and dreaming dreams of a life full of healthy children, healthy crops, and frequent visits with friends.

It turned out to be a financial disaster.

CHAPTER 12:

Disappointment, Joy, and Heartbreak

G rasshoppers are normally harmless, blending into the landscape with very little notice. Once in a while, though, due to climate conditions and/or extra moisture from irrigation or other factors, their breeding and eating habits change dramatically. They swarm. And they eat every green thing in sight.

That is what happened on the Noel farm in 1905. The air was a dark cloud of whirring, hungry insects. People sought shelter inside. The trees were stripped of leaves and fruit. The crops were gone. The garden was history. Nothing was left.

With a pregnant wife and three young children, Frank needed to find a job in a hurry.

On February 9. 1906, Mae gave birth to another son. They named him Henry Reginald after Frank's father and brother. They would call him Reginald.

With four children in six short years, God was certainly answering their prayers for children! Their two girls and two boys seemed just about perfect. But, with the farm a failure, they needed to figure out a way to earn money.

Joe Wilkins, the same man who had been instrumental in helping build up Two Grey Hills, had another trading post on the reservation and a logging contract on the mountain near his store. That summer, Frank went to work for him. He logged for him part of the year and worked in the store off and on the rest of the year. Tom Dustin, a friend from Fruitland, worked along-side him. Joe's wife, Lois, and their two children rented part of the house with Mae and the four Noel children.

Lois and Mae, living in the same space, had different parenting styles. Mae was reluctant to spank the children, preferring a kind of time-out discipline. Lois didn't mind spanking, thinking the children would remember better to avoid bad behavior. Sometimes the tension between them spilled over into other parts of the day. Still, the women usually enjoyed each other and made a good team as they helped each other with the six children.

But it was clear that Lois was not happy. She let her husband know that she would rather spend her time in Farmington with her circle of friends than on the reservation with the Navajos, who had ways she was not familiar with. Over time, it became clear that Joe Wilkins would have to do some-thing differently. He decided to sell his store.

There was another trader, C. H. Algert, who had moved from Tuba City, Arizona, and set up a large store in Fruitland. Frank met with him and told him he would like to buy the Wilkins store and have Algert's store as his supply house. Together, the two went to look over the Wilkins store and Algert agreed to loan Frank the money to buy it. He knew Frank had been in the business before, and he had come to trust him. Having Frank as a steady customer would be good for Algert's business. Getting the loan to start the store was a blessing to Frank. It was a win/win situation.

He called the store Sanostee, after the area where it was located, and took it over in 1906. In the meantime, Henry and Hambleton had sold Two Grey Hills, and Hambleton had already been staying at the Wilkins store off and on. So it became a family venture, with the three brothers working the store and Frank as the owner. As soon as the store was fully stocked, it started to make a profit. It proved to be one of the best financial moves of Frank's life.

Back home, however, Mae was not excited about the prospect of Frank being so far away again. She was taught to be supportive of whatever her husband decided to do to earn a living, and she *was* supportive. She also *missed* him. And when Lois and her children moved out, she was lonely.

Evidently, Frank was lonely too. Here is a letter he wrote to her when they were still thinking of buying the store.

Fruitland, N.M.

Sept. 29, 1905

Dear Dear Mary,

We are in camp today watching it rain with a wagon sheet over a pole for a tent & somebody is thinking about home &wishing he was there with the kids and the old lady. Why don't you write oftener sweetheart, you would if you knew how much I thought of your letters & how many times I read them.

Soxy if you only knew how much you are to me, & how fully you fill my Idea of a woman, you would be pleased. I am thankful I got a woman worthy of any one's respect. Now don't get conceited if you begin to know how dear you are to me, but I like to write what is on my mind, perhaps I am homesick.

Don is here & seems to like the work so I guess he will stay for a while anyway.

Am sorry you are having such a time there & know I ought to come in & help you, but you let everything go & don't worry so much, I am coming some of these days.

Joe will be back from Gallup today & I will send you some money as he will have some when he gets back.

You go to Algert & get some stuff for clothes for you & the kids & what you need to eat. Now Mary, get what you want & don't try to get along on nothing.

Hamp has made a deal with Joe to stay all winter so we will all have some money someday....

The store business better wait until next spring but if we have another winter that brings snow the Indians will have lots of stock & will be well off. Well, we have just had dinner and the rain is coming in sheets. If it clears up it will freeze here, what will I do without any one to sleep with, you better make up your mind to come out so a fellow can keep warm. Now Soxy, whenever you have a minute to spare just write to me. Kiss all the kids & yourself.

Your loving husband,
F. L. Noel (6)

Enough was enough. Frank missed her, and the Lord knew she missed him. So Mae hired a boy to go with her and the children to the reservation as a surprise for Frank. It just felt right to be together again, and they decided life was too short to be separated. Within a few short weeks, Mae and the children had all joined Frank and Hambleton at Sanostee. They were 30 miles from a settlement and 15 miles from the nearest neighbor. But they were together, and they were happy. The children had room to roam, and life was good again. The distance to town didn't matter.

Until it did.

In early August, little Leland, now 2 ½ years old, was just at that age when children are so cute you delight in just watching them. He could say a few words and communication was beginning to make sense. He could not only walk, but also spin around and jump with one foot at a time. Every new thing—every new bug, every new skill, every new cloud in the sky—was really, enthusiastically new. That's when little Leland contracted typhoid fever. Mae took him to her mother's house, where he could see a doctor. When he seemed well again, the doctor released him, and they went back to the reservation. Before long, Leland showed signs of relapsing. He had diarrhea, a swollen tummy, a rash, and he couldn't sleep. At times he seemed to be hallucinating. In short, he was miserable. Mae took him to the doctor in Shiprock, who gave them some medicine and sent them home again.

Leland continued to get worse.

Frank and Mae left the other children with a friend and headed out toward Durango where they knew they could get the best care. They decided to stop in Farmington. Perhaps the trip was too hard on Leland, and they were afraid to go on. Perhaps they remembered good things about the doctors in Farmington. At any rate, they stayed, prayed fervently, watched him constantly, and did everything that could be done. But to no avail.

Their first son, sweet little Frank Leland Noel, passed away on Wednesday, November 28, 1906. He was buried in the Fruitland Cemetery the next day… Thanksgiving Day.

The following day, Frank and Mae turned toward home and their other children with breaking hearts. They knew that nothing and no one would ever replace their little Leland. Not work, not prayer, not time, and not the new baby that was soon to be born to them.

Mae determined to trust God, even when she didn't understand what He was doing. What else could she do? She tried to picture her sweet little boy in heaven with a new assignment, a new purpose that she would understand in time.

Frank was numb. Then he was angry. Why? There wasn't a single other case of typhoid around. Why did it come to Leland? Why weren't the doctors able to save him? Why didn't all of those prayers save him? But "why" was never answered. Frank felt as he did when his mother passed away. They had done everything humanly possible. In addition to doing what the doctors said, they had begged God for the life of someone they cherished. It hadn't helped his mother, and it hadn't helped his son. All of those prayers had resulted in nothing but despair and a huge hole in his heart.

In his own words, *A man at such times loses all his faith in a belief that our lives are all directed; he is a changed man. He loses all direction in which way to turn and what to believe next. Time and work are his only comforts.*

Also in his words, *What saved me in the second great crisis of my life was my wife and family. She was the strong character who never wavered, that still kept her faith, and in the end saved me, and led the family along a Christian life. But for her comfort and happiness in our family the present would certainly have been impossible.* (4)

Knowing she had to prepare for another baby very soon, Mae set about making their home ready. When her time was close, Frank took her to her mother and headed back to take care of the other children. He promised to stop in Shiprock to hear if there was any news. There was.

On January 7, 1907, their daughter Mary was born. Named for her mother and grandmother, Mary had the sweet spirit of both. The doctor was called.

but didn't make it in time. Frank turned back from Shiprock as soon as he got the message, but Mary was already born when he arrived. He called her "my boy" for a while. Mae called her delivery, with only her mother present, a miracle.

After a few days, Frank went home to take care of the other children, and a neighbor, Emma Nelson, took Reginald, now just under a year old, to be with Mae and his new little sister. In the middle of February, they returned home. Home again, where Mae could watch all the children popping corn or apples in the fireplace in the evening. Home again, where she could open the door between their living room and the store and watch her husband hard at work. She let out a deep breath and smiled.

It didn't last.

It wasn't long before it was clear that Mae again needed a doctor. She and Frank made plans to take the two youngest babies and set out for Shiprock. When they got to the San Juan River, it was running dangerously high. It wasn't unheard of for horses and wagons to be swept downriver in conditions like that. But they had to get across and, to do that, they had to concentrate on each step forward. Frank hired a Navajo man to help by carrying Reginald, while Mae clung to Mary. But Reginald was afraid of the Native and started to cry. The undaunted Native swept him up in his blanket, put him on his back and started soothing him in Navajo. Reginald was too startled to make a sound. They crossed safely.

When they saw the doctor in Shiprock, they were told Mae would need to stay for treatment. But there were no rooms readily available. Searching, Frank finally found a room next to a little store. It was small, very dirty, barely furnished, and decidedly uninviting. But it was a room.

After Frank went back to the other children, Mae began to clean. She couldn't even see out of the window, so she started with that. Then she tackled the pile of cans in the corner and was relieved when a friend, Mr.

Hubbard, showed up with a shovel and a wheelbarrow. His wife sent clean sheets for the bed and a small lamp. The landlady started to relax and become more pleasant when she saw the changes and saw Mae spending money in her store. But she was shocked when Henry showed up with Clara and Jennie to stay there too. The men were finding it hard to watch the store and two young children at the same time. There were now four children in that little space, and the oldest was six. Mae asked Mr. Hubbard to make another little bed for them, and they passed the time reading stories, playing games, and going for walks among the hills.

Eventually, although she was not completely well, Mae sent for Frank to come and get them and bring them home. No release from the doctor. No miraculous healing. She just wanted to go home.

CHAPTER 13:

On The Reservation

Being an Indian trader could be dangerous work. Frank took over Sanostee a year after the U.S. Government declared sovereignty over the Native populations. An underlying tension was felt throughout the region. There were lots of stories about traders who had been killed when they were alone in their stores, stories of all the goods being taken and the stores burned to the ground. At the same time, there were also plenty of stories about men who thought they had the right to tell Native Americans how to live. Laws were imposed that made no sense in their culture. Children were taken out of their homes and put in government schools that had horrible reputations. Many promises were made with no intention of honoring them. Learning to trust, on either side, was not easy.

The first time Frank met Chief Bizhoshi, Frank had just killed the chief's dog. There had been some squawking from the henhouse, so Frank grabbed his rifle and went to check it out. He got there in time to see a strange dog killing one of his chickens. Without a second thought, he shot and killed the dog. Soon after that, the medicine man, who lived nearby, came up to the store, so mad he was shaking. Hambleton warned Frank to step lightly. The medicine man was an important person in the tribe, and he was obviously angry. Bizhoshi immediately started yelling at Frank that he had needed that dog to guard his sheep and goats from coyotes. This was

his land and Frank had to go —**immediately**. When it was Frank's turn to talk, he explained that he had thought it was a rogue dog, killing anything it came across, and that he was doing the whole community a favor by killing it. Since it belonged to the medicine man, Frank offered to pay for the dog. He put some flour, sugar, coffee, and tobacco on the counter with $2 cash, hoping it was an acceptable price for the dog. He waited to see if his offer would be accepted.

Finally, it was. The men shook hands and Bizhoshi said *sakisagay*, meaning "friend.". It would prove to be an important alliance.

Chief Bizhoshi Source: Private collection

Business was good at Sanostee. Hambleton had become very good at judging the quality of Navajo blankets and, before long, weavers were coming long distances to sell their blankets. Often, they would camp outside the store. A hogan was built for them, and the Noel brothers furnished them with wood, flour, and coffee. When the quality of the blankets reached the outside world, customers also began traveling long distances to see them.

Navajo blankets on display from Sanostee Source: 80 Years in America

Mae and the children got used to seeing Navajos around the store on a daily basis. They were inside, trading goods and chatting, or outside, camping and cooking. They were an ever-present part of the landscape. After all, they were on a reservation. This was nothing new for Mae. She had spent years at Two Grey Hills, trading with Natives there. For the children, it was how they grew up, and so was a normal part of life for them too. No concerns.

As the children were growing older, the Noels developed a plan of the family being together at the store in the summer. Then Mae would take the children to the home in Fruitland for the school year. After one year of that, they hired a teacher to come and live with them on the reservation.

The only time they used the home in Fruitland for very long was when another baby was born.

During the school year, when the family was gone, Frank really needed something to do besides work. The weekdays were an endless cycle of working in the store all day and sleeping at night, just to go back to the same thing the next day. The government required them to be closed on Sundays. Sundays. So, Frank bought a couple of greyhounds, and on Sundays he would get his horse, call to his dogs, and go hunting jackrabbits. Knowing that his dogs hunted more by visual cues than anything else, he would take them to some flat area and turn them loose. Frank would wait with the horse on a little ridge somewhere nearby and watch the dogs. He could always tell when they found a rabbit, and he could always tell what the rabbit was doing by watching the dogs. When both dogs were chasing a rabbit, he would urge his horse into the race. The dogs and the rabbit could outrun the horse, but he watched for the rabbit to circle back to its hole and cut them off. The closer the dogs got to the rabbit, the closer their noses got to the ground. Normally, when the dog caught a rabbit, it was one snap of the neck, and it was all over. The funny thing about it was that no one made a sound. The rabbit, the dogs, the horse, the man were all too intent on the chase to waste the energy. That was very different from the noisy fox hunts he had watched at Paynefield. Now, when they caught a rabbit, instead of a loud celebration, they would all just take a short rest and try for one more before heading home.

Sometimes, he would be invited to watch the Navajos hunt rabbits. No dogs. No saddles. No guns. Decidedly, no silence in the hunt. Just 12 to 30 riders on their best horses, around a ridge surrounding a flat plain, with water running through and high brush where the rabbits could hide. When everyone was in place, an older man would ride whooping and shouting through the middle of the brush and scare out a rabbit. Each hunter prepared to ride in case the rabbit came their way. When it did, a rider chased it until it came back toward their circle. That rider would stop, and a fresh rider would take up the chase. That might happen two or three times, with a fresh rider chasing each time the rabbit turned. When it tried to sprint toward its home, one of the riders close to the brush would hit it with a club and knock it out.

This continued until the horses were tired and they had 10 to 30 rabbits to share. Then they would saddle their horses and head to the trading post. The women normally went ahead and were given coffee and flour. As they all feasted, they would retell the stories of the hunt, laughing and reenacting the highlights.

In good years, there were many opportunities to enjoy celebrations with their Navajo friends. In addition to rabbit hunts, there were horse races, and ceremonial dances when several villages came together and danced for days. The memories of those times made Frank smile years later, too.

In the summer, Sundays meant Sunday school classes for the children, then exploring through the hills. They came across caves, found petroglyphs, collected interesting rocks, and visited their Navajo friends. After the day when Mae nearly got bitten by a huge rattlesnake, they also kept an eye out for snakes. They all came to know and love the desert as their home.

Chief Bizhoshi continued to be a good customer and a good friend.

CHAPTER 14:

Relief

In March of 1908, it was time to pack up the children and move, once again, into the house in Fruitland. Another baby was on the way, and Frank hired someone to take his place in the store, while he saw the family safely back.

The day they were to leave, a huge snowstorm came through. The wind was blowing, and they could barely see the path ahead. The horses were having trouble making their way through the snowdrifts. They were reluctant to go on, but knew they didn't have a choice. They drove the wagon into an arroyo, where they would be protected from the wind, fed the children, bundled up again, and headed out once more.

What a welcome sight it was when they arrived to find a clean house, a warm fire, and a friend who would be with Mae until their baby was born!

Curly-haired and blue-eyed little Bessie Noel was born on March 19, 1908, to a family that cherished her, knowing she was an answer to prayer.

Relief Society

With three children under three and two old enough to be in school, it was clear to Mae that she needed some time in town.

Once there, with her hands more than full, she was nominated for president of the Relief Society in Fruitland. She told Frank she wasn't sure why she would be nominated. There were older, more experienced women around who had grown children. But Frank said that, if she agreed to do it, he would support her as long as she held that office, and he did.

Being the president of the Relief Society meant that she would hold regular meetings, visit the women of her church, and tend to their spiritual needs, as well as provide teaching, emotional support, and help in times of need. Mae loved it.

She traveled with her friend, Villa Collyer, each taking her babies with her as they visited other women from the church. Before long they had a group of women who would meet together to sew skirts, quilts, and rugs. These handcrafted items were sold at Sanostee and in town, and the money helped them continue their work in the community. Frank continued to support them by sending bolts of fabric, and the women never lacked for something to do.

The meetings were generally well-received and well-attended. Mae and Villa made up their minds that the meetings would happen on a regular basis, no matter what. So in the summer, when it was too hot and attendance dropped severely, they would go across the street and bring back a friend who was blind. She felt safe with just two other women, and she made the third person needed to constitute an official Relief Society meeting.

On the anniversary of the Relief Society, they put on a big party and the whole community came. Everyone brought food. Tables were stacked high with chicken, turkey, ham, roast beef, pies, cakes, jams, and jellies. Homemade ice cream was plentiful.

Another time, they needed to do a fundraiser. They decided to have all of the ladies prepare picnic baskets for the men to bid on... without being able to see what was inside! This was a widespread practice at the time. The baskets and food were donated, and all of the money went to the needs of the Relief Society. It was fun to see how each basket was decorated and to guess what was inside. Many of the men bought more than one basket, to be sure they had enough food to share and to support the Relief Society. The ladies felt really proud if the bidding on their baskets kept going up. One lady who came from Sweden made her husband promise to buy her basket because, she said, none of the other men would want her cooking. To her delight the bidding kept going up, forcing her husband to spend $5 to keep his promise! Frank bought Mae's basket and another one for good measure. When he was overheard saying he wished he had bought a third basket, because neither of his contained lemon pie, a helpful person brought him a nice big slice of lemon pie from their own basket. That made him smile... until he tasted it. Did they leave out the sugar? It wasn't what he had hoped for, but the gift was still appreciated.

Through the Relief Society, Mae learned first-hand that, when God calls you to do something, He will provide you with what you need to do the job... even if what you are missing is simply stamina.

Their time in Fruitland created many good memories. The people were not rich, but not poor either. They worked hard, took care of each other, and instilled in their children a very positive idea of what a community should be.

And there were more blessings.

On June 11, 1909, Floyd Noel was born. His parents were happy that Reginald had a brother to grow up with. They thought of their seventh child as a special blessing. He grew up knowing he was wanted and loved.

They remembered praying that God would allow them to be parents. He was answering their prayer with a resounding "Yes!" As it turns out, God can be very generous.

Frank came and went during those days, running the store when it needed him, coming to town when he could. Mae also came and went during those days. She stayed primarily in town but would pack everyone up when she needed Frank's help in parenting, craved a shoulder to lean on, or just plain missed him.

The following spring and summer were busy. There were now four children under four and Mae found herself frequently asking nine-year-old Clara to help out. "Clara, run and get me diapers." "Clara, please run and get the baby out of the cupboard." "Clara, please run and close the door. Bessie is trying to get out." "Mama, can I *walk* just one time, please?"

Six-year-old Jennie was also pressed into service, skillfully watching the little ones when Mae needed to be busy with cooking or laundry or mending clothes.

Mae soon began to put into practice the training she received as a kindergarten teacher years earlier. She could often be found teaching songs, marching, stringing beads, sorting, and generally holding a class with her own children.

No amount of distraction, however, would hide the fact that Floyd was teething and very sick. Mae didn't feel well either, and the hotter it got, the more they were pestered with flies from the river near their home. It was becoming unbearable.

When Frank came, he could see how miserable they were, and decided it was time for another mountain break. Mae's sister Daphne and brother-in-law Roy had a sheep camp up in the Colorado mountains. They could go there. They bought a tent and excitedly started getting ready for their trip. Daphne and Roy decided to go up and stay in their cabin at the same time. Their two cows and their milk proved to be a lifesaver for little Floyd.

Frank stayed long enough to get everyone settled and enjoy his family for a few days. When he had to go back, the family entertained themselves by watching men shoeing horses and mules, tending sheep, telling stories around the campfire at night, exploring the flowers and tall trees that grew there, and playing in the little stream that ran near the tent. Each child was growing up with an appreciation of nature that would last their whole lives. They stayed there a month.

When it was time to go back to Fruitland, Frank came to get them, and they packed everything up to head down the mountain. Once home, Mae was feeling stronger and more relaxed. She cleaned the house, put the girls in school, and started Relief Society again. Frank stayed on; they were expecting another baby and he wanted to be there for the birth.

Wright Noel was born November 10, 1910. Named after Frank's brother and uncle, Wright was born a tiny little thing. His parents were delighted with another son, and Wright grew up knowing he was dearly loved.

CHAPTER 15:

Beginning of Trouble

Tensions had been increasing between the government and the tribes for years. The Homestead Act was allowing settlers to claim large tracts of land which the Native Americans considered their home. Then, in 1905, the U.S. Government claimed jurisdiction over the Native people. As the white man continued to impose his will and his ways on the Native way of life, some of the Native leaders were refusing to comply. While things remained friendly at Sanostee, everyone was aware of the underlying tension.

William Shelton was superintendent of Indian Affairs in the Shiprock office. He was a man who had little respect for the Native way of life, viewing them as uneducated and sometimes dangerous. At the same time, he had a great deal of respect for his own education and position with the government. Surely, he thought, he was a man who could compel the Navajos in his jurisdiction to become educated and civilized. He would get the job done.

Years before, in the fall of 1907, Superintendent Shelton issued an order that all Navajo children in his area would attend the boarding school at Shiprock. This practice had been adopted in other areas for about 10 years. On the one side, the government claimed they were in the right because they were educating children and introducing them to Christianity and the civilized world. They would not take "no" for an answer. On the other side, the Navajos resented the move to erase their culture. They had been warned about the overcrowding, poor food, and abusive practices at some of those schools, and they were determined to protect their children. The order did not go over well.

Byalille, a medicine man and chief of the area, flatly refused to allow the children of his tribe to be taken. Superintendent Shelton called for backup for his position, and before long about 75 calvary from Fort Wingate were on their way to enforce his order. On October 29. 1907, they surrounded Byalille's camp around daybreak. One member of the tribe came out of his hogan with a rifle, and shot at one of the troopers, killing his horse. As soon as he shot, the calvary opened fire, and soon two of the tribesmen were dead. Byalille was handcuffed and arrested. On the way to the jail at Shiprock, the soldiers and prisoners camped overnight at Sanostee. The Navajos at Frank's store had never seen a U.S. soldier. They could see that the medicine man was handcuffed to a Navajo policeman, but no one was allowed to talk to them about what they were seeing. It was unnerving, to say the least. The Navajos around Sanostee would talk about this and remember it for years.

These government schools, in both the United States and Canada would become infamous. More than 100 years later, we are still learning of horrible abuses, hundreds of unmarked graves of children whose parents were never notified of their deaths, and negative social practices that have impacted generations of Native people. One woman reports the beatings children received if they did not "profess Christ." Amazingly, this ordeal did not turn her away from Jesus. It did teach her to get her way using physical force and manipulation… and to mistrust all clergy.

In April of 1908, Brigadier General Hugh Scott, head of West Point, called on missionary Anselm Weber to further investigate what happened. *In the discussion with Scott the missioner again stresses the fact that though Superintendent Shelton was an excellent agriculturist he was not the administrator type suited to handle Indians, nor could he be generally upheld in the*

Aneth fracas [the incident involving Byalille]. *The friar admitted that there was widespread discontent among the Indians of Shelton's jurisdiction. For the good of Government-Indian relations, Father Anselm believed, Mr. Shelton should be replaced.* (10, pg. 180)

He was not.

In 1910, the Natives knew him by reputation, and they did not trust him. Shelton's heavy-handed approach was well-known throughout the region. According to historian Frank McNitt, *Shelton was a hard disciplinarian, a stubborn man who would tolerate no opposition to his methods. All Navaho were unruly children, Shelton believed... and so, the rod was applied frequently. An empty jailhouse was a sign of laxity, so the agency police worked overtime, and the jail scarcely ever wanted for tenants.* (10, pg. 345) Byalille and another of his clan were sentenced to 10 years' hard labor in Alcatraz without a trial.

CHAPTER 16:

1911 – Historic Flood

S helton did have some redeeming moments as superintendent. For example, in 1909he started an annual fair in Shiprock. The fair was a place where the Navajos were encouraged to bring the best of their goods to sell, and people came from miles around to see their livestock and their beautiful blankets, rugs, and jewelry. This resulted in an exchange of ideas among the villages, which increased the value of the market. It also brought more and more non-Natives out to see what they were missing. Traders, too, brought their best goods to showcase at the Shiprock Fair. The people loved it.

Navajo women and children and Sanostee display at Shiprock Fair 80 Years in America

But even Shelton's good ideas had to be on his own terms, no matter the cost.

In October of 1911, Frank was preparing to set up a booth at the Shiprock Fair. He asked Mae to go with him. They would get someone to watch the children and enjoy the fair together. It would be fun.

It was, at least, memorable.

> *The rain began in the San Juan Mountains late on the morning of October 4, 1911. It came down gently at first, slowly gaining intensity over the course of the day. By evening the tropical storm was a torrent, dropping two inches of precipitation on Durango in just 12 hours, nearly twice what the town normally gets during all of October. Weather watchers in Gladstone, above Silverton, recorded eight inches of rain on October 5—a virtual high-country hurricane, (8)*

Meanwhile, Frank and other traders were setting up their booths at the Indian Fair in Shiprock. It had been raining off and on for a couple of weeks. Still, they camped on the river bottom that was normally dry at this time of year. Exhibit booths were set up on higher ground. The rain continued. When the river rose the second night, Frank, Hambleton, and other campers moved up on a hill. The next morning, when they went to check on their horses, they found the water up to the horses' backs. Scared horses were straining to keep their noses above water. They moved the horses immediately, and asked Shelton's permission to move the exhibits to higher ground. He refused.

Frank got a message from a friend upriver that the Cherry Creek reservoir above Durango had broken. The water was cresting and was already up to his door. A flood was coming. The campers decided to do the smart thing. Defying Shelton, they moved up and out of harm's way. When the river crested at Shiprock hours later, the San Juan bridge and the exhibits were swept away. Houses closer to the river had water up to the eaves. It was, and still is, the worst flood in the history of the valley.

Animas River Peak Annual Streamflow 1898-2016

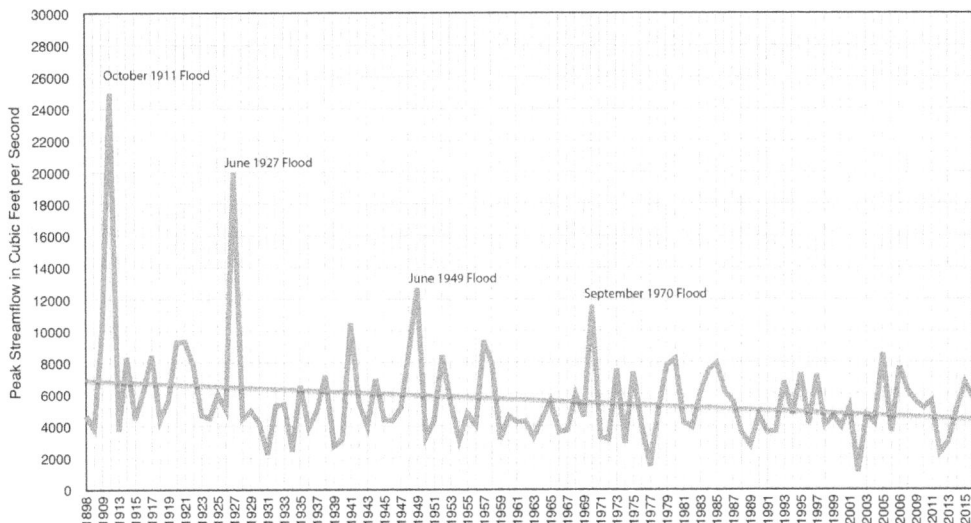

October 1911 Flood

June 1927 Flood

June 1949 Flood

September 1970 Flood

Source: (8) **River of Lost Souls**

All thoughts of a good time vanished. Their thoughts went immediately to their children. Had the flood waters reached their house? Were the children safe? There was no way to know. It was too dark and too dangerous to try to go back until daylight. All they could do was pray that God would protect the children and their friend, Mamie, who was watching them.

The next day, as soon as she could, Mae caught a ride with a couple going back home. They rode next to the river over 20 miles, and sometimes the water was so high on the road that it reached the bed of their buggy. It was slow-going, and what they saw as they made their way did nothing to calm their fears. Mae watched as everything that wasn't tied down floated passedthem: branches, trees, furniture, small animals, even small houses. But there was no turning back. She worried about her children, her own house, her own animals.

Fortunately, Mamie's father, knowing they were dangerously close to the river, immediately rushed to take them to higher ground. They hurriedly put their bedding in the wagon, and he took them to Mae's sister-in-law,

Mary Roberts, who welcomed them with open arms. There was no room in the main part of the house for everyone, but the children slept safely in the Roberts' attic that night.

When Mae found her children safe and had her baby in her arms, she nearly collapsed with relief.

Thank you, Lord!

Grateful that the children were alive and safe, she slowly realized she might not have a place to take them. Their home might be so flooded that they would never be able to stay there. Where could they go?

Frank and Mae had rented two rooms about a mile away for her parents to live in, but they hadn't moved in yet. So she took the children there. She stopped and bought some tin dishes and food and hired someone to take her purchases to the rooms. There was no furniture, so they just put their quilts on the floor and tried to take stock of what to do next. Later in the day, her sister, Daphne, and Daphne's husband, Roy, brought Frank from Shiprock, and they all collapsed on the floor, grateful to be alive and together.

The next day, Frank hired a boat and went out to see what was left of their home. He was amazed to find it still standing. Some chicken wire around the garden had served to catch a lot of the floating debris. This, in turn, split the flow of the river around their house. There was about a foot of water in it, but it was still standing. The animals fared better than expected, too. Their pig and most of the chickens were gone, somewhere downstream. But some of the chickens had roosted above the water. The cows were standing near the chicken coop in water up to their bellies. Frank took feed out to them in the boat. They needed milking badly and they were hungry, but no worse for wear. The ducks, of course, were happily swimming around, thrilled to have so much water and wondering what the fuss was all about.

It was a full month before the water receded enough for them to get into the house. They found floors covered in mud and some damage from the water, but all of their furniture was still in the house. A mountain of work waited for them to make the house livable again. But they were grateful for what was there, knowing what they lost could someday be replaced, and knowing some were not so lucky.

Their neighbors, the Collyers, found it hard to believe the flood that was coming was going to be any worse than it had been before. Cyril Collyer was in his garden when he looked up and saw a wall of water coming at him. He screamed for his wife to get the children in the wagon, and he headed for the barn to get the horses. It was almost too late. As they headed over the bridge, it gave way and floated downstream. He finally got the wagon onto higher ground. They were all safe. But the house had been left open, and they spent the next several weeks collecting furniture, bedding, clothes, and dishes from trees, bushes, and all along the ground.

CHAPTER 17:

A Thief in the Night

That fall hit the Noel children like a sledgehammer. Five of the seven got whooping cough, and all of them had pinkeye. Mae put cold cloths around their necks to relieve the cough and fever, and eventually arranged the beds in a kind of semicircle so she could reach each one easily. Jennie and Reginald were the only ones who didn't get whooping cough. But Jennie had croup and Reginald didn't feel well either. Seven children, and all of them were sick. In addition to soothing feverish heads and trying to be encouraging, there were still meals to prepare, clothes and bedding to wash by hand, and the fire to keep going. Frank was working at the store, so he wasn't able to help at all. It was exhausting. As many times as they had been separated, it seemed to Mae that she should have a system in place. It was supposed to be easier than it was. But her system didn't account for **all** of the children being sick at the same time. She hardly slept. She did hire a young girl to help her, but she wasn't much help. Ice was already forming on the water outside. Winter was coming, and Mae was just about at her wits' end.

Eventually, she got word that there was a phone call from Frank. She walked the half-mile to the nearest phone, excited to hear that he would soon be home to help her. Instead, when she called him back, he told her he had to make another trip for more cattle. He was delayed.

Delayed? For more cattle? She couldn't believe what she was hearing! She desperately needed his help. She needed to hear that he was coming soon, or that he was already on his way. Exhausted and angry, she couldn't put on a brave face any longer. When he asked how the children were doing, she snapped, "What difference does it make? They will either be dead or well when you get back." Then she hung up the phone and paced the half-mile back to their sick children.

That night, around midnight, Frank rode into the yard. He must have started for home as soon as he heard the frustration in Mae's voice. It was a good decision.

Mae came down with pneumonia the very next day, and Frank was able to take over.

He hired a young woman to come and stay with them, specifically to take care of Mae. He took over the children, and stayed several weeks, until Mae was completely well again. Then he went back to the store and didn't come home again until Christmas.

It was a hard winter. The children were frequently sick, possibly because of all the spores that lingered in their recently flooded home. Mae started feeling the effects of rheumatism. She was always tired. No, she was literally exhausted!

Relief Society

In the spring, the Relief Society decided to help. A friend came down one day and spent the day cutting out clothes for all of the growing children. The next day, all of the ladies got together and sewed all day long. By the end of the day, there were new clothes for all of the children from their skin out. They had new underwear, petticoats, dresses, shirts, and pants.

Mae had spent years doing things like this for other people through her own work in the Relief Society. This was the first time she was on the receiving end. She was humbled and at the same time overcome with gratitude. She thanked God for her friends and knew that she would do more focused work in the future, knowing what it was like to be on both sides of God's provision.

Mae was sick all the next summer, too. When Frank took her to the doctor, they were told that she needed an operation for a growth. But Mae didn't want the operation. She knew she carried the majority of the weight for the day-to-day lives of their seven children. She couldn't imagine things running smoothly if she took that much time off again. She prayed for guidance and went to Bishop Nielson and Newell R. Young for a blessing. They assured her that, if her faith was strong enough, she would be healed. Did she have that much faith? When she told Frank what they had said, he responded, "Of course you have it. If you haven't, I have." That was music to her ears.

That day she received word that the women of the church were fasting and praying for her. She was invited to join them. So she fasted and prayed, too, and went to the meeting. The women all told their own stories of God's provision. Then two of them put their hands on Mae's head and gave her a blessing, promising she would be made whole. Mae immediately felt at peace, and a warmth throughout her whole body. She knew that she would be fine.

The growth the doctors were planning to operate on dissolved that night. There was no fanfare, no meaningful rupture in her body. It was simply gone.

With that scare behind them, Frank and Mae decided that, from now on, they needed to be together as a family all year long. Mae and the children moved to Sanostee; and her Navajo friends were delighted to see her back.

Frank owned a second store about 30 miles away, on the road to Gallup. Charlie Nelson ran that store, and one of his sons, who spoke Navajo well, was a perfect choice to work at the counter there. Charlie's wife and younger children lived in a tent at Sanostee, happy to have other children around. They joined their little Sunday school classes, with Frank taking the older children and Mae taking the younger ones. Sometimes, after Sunday school, they took their donkey and a picnic basket into the hills. There was often a campfire where they cooked bacon and eggs and potatoes, and the children loved it.

In the fall, they hired Sarah Young to stay at the store and teach school. Sarah brought her two children with her, so the house was definitely filling up. But life at Sanostee took on a pleasant rhythm again, and everyone seemed content.

As Christmas of 1912 approached, they became very familiar with the Sears and Roebuck catalog. They ordered their tree and some treats for the younger children. The older children were kept busy decorating. They trimmed the tree, made paper garlands, and popped popcorn in the fireplace. It was beginning to feel like home.

Two things kept it from being perfect.

Frank developed trachoma, an eye disease that can be very serious if left untreated. Some Sundays he would head out early to the doctor in Shiprock, 30 miles away. The doctor would paint his eyelids with a mixture of some kind, and he would need to stay put with a cold cloth on his eyes until the sun went down. Then he would ride the 30 miles back home to be ready for the store the next day. They were long days.

The other thing that kept things from being perfect was that they were robbed. Someone broke into the store and took a lot of money and some of the goods. There was no clear culprit, so they began to wonder and question. It was always at the back of their minds.

The last week of January, Mae went to Farmington to await the arrival of another child. When she got to town, she looked up her doctor and he immediately invited her to wait at his home with him and his wife. She only waited three days. On February 1, 1913, she welcomed another son and named him Howard, in memory of the brother she had lost to drowning in the San Juan River years before. She sang to him and told him stories of his uncle and what a friendly and happy man he was. She prayed that her son would grow to be just such a man. He certainly captured the hearts of the doctor and his wife.

When Howard was nine days old, they left the doctor and moved in with Hambleton for a few days. They were to stay with him until Mae was well enough to travel. But Howard developed colic, and Mae spent most nights trying to comfort him and keep him quiet enough so Hambleton could sleep. Finally, the doctor suggested she go home where she could have more help.

They were enthusiastically welcomed back. Everyone was eager to meet Baby Howard and very glad to see Mae again. She was grateful to Sarah Young for having done her best to keep up with the teaching, the children, and the house while she was gone. Sarah was becoming a very good friend, but there was one incident that almost spoiled the relationship.

The store was robbed again.

Frank began to wonder if it was Sarah. After all, with just a door separating the home from the store, she had access to the store at any time. Who else had that much opportunity?

Mae was sure Sarah was innocent. Sarah, for her part, refused to come out of her room once Mae was home, unable to function with the accusations hanging in the air. Finally, Mae asked her permission to search through her things, assuring her she wasn't accusing her, but only wanted to prove her innocence. They searched together and nothing turned up. But with accusations still hanging in the air, tensions remained.

Finally, Mae asked Sarah to take a walk with her in the hills where they could be alone and no one but God could hear their conversation. It was a strategy that worked with Frank. Why not a lady friend? When they were sure to be alone, they got down on their knees and prayed that God would clear the air between them. Sarah needed to be convinced that Mae did not accuse her. Mae needed to be sure of the best way to address the whole situation with her husband. When they got up from their knees, there was peace between them, and they knew they would always rely on that peace.

Now that Sarah had been cleared, and there was no other obvious suspect, Frank and Mae examined every possibility. There were two windows in the door. Could someone come in that way? The windows were just openings with no glass. Frank thought the windows were too small, but, just to be sure, he took down the door and added iron bars across the windows. Time went on.

The third time, the thief left a trail. He climbed in through a higher window, and when he climbed out, he dropped a lot of the silver he had stolen. Frank took one of the Nelson boys and a Navajo man by the name of Wilson, and they set out to find the culprit. They found fresh horse tracks that had been left during the night, and Wilson made an impression. One of the horse's hooves was broken.

They followed the trail of the broken hoof over the hills.

Meanwhile, Mae and Jennie were doing some washing that day when the wind came up. Mae was afraid the wind would blow the tracks away and the men would not be able to find the thief. So she took Jennie, now 10, into a tent alone, and they prayed that God would stop the wind until the culprit was caught.

When Frank and his friends caught up with the thief, it was a Navajo youth who had seen his chance and taken it. After he got away with stealing once, he was tempted to go again and then again. The third time, he had to find another way in because the window in the door was barred. But he was determined, and this time he left enough evidence to implicate himself.

The young man's father was embarrassed for his son, and helped Frank dig up the stolen goods. They were in a tin can buried in the floor of their hogan.

When Frank returned with his stolen merchandise, Jennie, curious about how things happened, asked her father if the wind had caused them any trouble with tracking the thief. "No, Honey," he said; "the wind didn't start until we reached the hogan." Jennie couldn't help but smile.

Frank was very pleased to be able to tell Sarah, and anyone else who felt they were under suspicion, that the case was finally solved. They didn't need to worry about it anymore.

The young thief went to jail. When he had served his term, he came back to Sanostee and asked if they could put the past behind them.

CHAPTER 18:

Beautiful Mountain War

O n August 26, 1913, a Navajo man reported that his wife had been killed by a medicine man. Superintendent Shelton, the same Superintendent Shelton who refused to authorize moving their goods when a flood was coming, investigated. The investigation turned up no evidence of liability on the part of the medicine man, and the case was dismissed. What it did turn up, though, sparked an episode that captured the attention of the entire nation.

*Hatali Yazhe Source: (5) **Along Navaho Trails***

Hatali Yazhe, also known as Little Singer—son of Bizhoshi, friend of Frank Noel, and a medicine man in his own right—had three wives. Polygamy was illegal, but it was widely practiced in the Navajo culture at that time, as a way of taking care of widows and single women. In this case, one report states that Hatali Yazhe was a widower who wanted to remarry. When he proposed, his intended refused unless he also married her mother and sister. (8)

Many families, both Navajo and Mormon, included more than one wife long before the United States Government declared that polygamy was illegal. How it was handled largely depended on the local government. In some cases, men were expected to choose one wife and put the rest aside. In other cases, the families were left intact with strict orders not to take on any more wives in the future.

Superintendent Shelton sent one of his Navajo policemen to bring in Hatali Yazhe and his wives for a talk. Yazhe was out hunting and not available, so the policeman brought in the three wives and held them in custody until Hatali Yazhe could come in for questioning. Chief Bizhoshi went along, too, and said he would see that his son came in to talk. Not trusting that Hatali Yazhe would come, Shelton retained the wives, and put them to work in the school garden.

Reports get a little murky here. Some reports suggest the women were jailed as opposed to being set to work. The important thing is that the wives were detained against their will.

That did not go over well with Hatali Yazhe. On September 17, he and 11 other men rode to the school at Shiprock, located the wives, and forcibly took them home again. Here are two versions of what happened.

Will Evans was a trader in the area and well acquainted with the other traders and many of the Navajos. His version is:

Little Singer [Hatali Yazhe] and a band of Navajos crossed the river at Shiprock. Galloping, whooping, and firing their rifles and pistols into the air as they entered the agency grounds. Superintendent William T. Shelton was away on business; there were no armed guards, and only Sephus Jensen, the agency farmer, Mr. Hinds, the clerk, and a policeman called Lame One [Na'rishod] were there. These men rushed out of the office building to meet the oncoming raiders, but their efforts were futile. One of them grabbed the bridle reins of Old School Boy's [Olta'iSani] horse, but the rider whipped him with a quirt and forced him to turn loose. Little Singer beat Mr. Hinds with a riding quirt, while a Navajo named Luce whipped and dragged around Lame One. Any witnesses soon fled for refuge in the buildings.

The three women, one of whom had a baby, were prisoners at the agency. They had been given the peaceful occupation of hoeing in the gardens until Little Singer was captured and brought in. At this time, two of them were in the garden plot hoeing, while the one with the baby, Luce's sister, sat at the front of the jail which was jokingly called the Department of Justice. During the melee, Luce rode his pony and led a bare-backed horse to his sister, grabbed her and the baby, hastily placed them on the spare pony, and told her to ride home as fast as she could. The other two women mounted horses, the group crossed the bridge, and disappeared in the desert toward Sanostee Valley. Jensen, Hinds, and Lame One could not stop them. (9 pgs. 93-94).

Chief Bizhoshi was there. This account was given by him to Superintendent Peter Paquette and Father Anselm Weber on November 1, 1913, six weeks after the incident:

We did not intend when we started to have war or have a fight. We camped on the side of the San Juan. I said we would go to the Superintendent and beg four times for the children and women before we would take any steps. Early in the day we rode up to the San Juan School. All the young fellows were ahead. When I overtook the young

*men, they were all in front of the police quarters, but he [a policeman]
did not answer me where they [the women] were. I asked the policeman
why he had taken them to the Agency.*

*The Clerk would not let us take the women. I begged him to let us [have]
the women. I told him we would camp in front of the store. We would
take the women over there and get them something to eat. The Clerk
said no. I asked him eight times. I told him we would go over by the store
to wait for Mr. Shelton to come back but the Clerk would not listen to us.
We got the women out. One of the women ran toward where we went
to go. We put one of the women on a horse. We went out the same way
we came in. It was the road toward the store. When we went out that
way there were some white people and some school children blocking
the way so we could not get out. Then I rode up and asked them to let
us pass on and stay in front of the store until Mr. Shelton got back, but
they would not open the way for us. They blocked the way, so I rode
among the crowd and one of the white men, a farmer, got hold of my
bridle rein. Another called "Yellow Man" [Jensen] got hold of the rein
on the other side and would not let us go. We found there were only
two policemen there. All at once one of the policemen jumped one of
our men. I got hold of this fellow. I got hold of the policeman's wrist
and held the policeman's hand. I then began whipping my horse. One
of the white men, a farmer, tried to stop me. He is just about as ugly
as I am. I ran my horse through the crowd. Some of the young fellows
whipped the policeman. The white people did not do anything at all....*

*I do not think we have done anything wrong. They came and stole our
women; we stole them back. (9, pgs. 248-249)*

So there are two very different perspectives. But the fact remains that the
women were taken against their will, then taken back, to some degree forcibly, by their friends and family.

Shelton's reaction to this was to write to District Attorney Burkhart, asking him to swear out an arrest warrant for each of the men involved. He said they should be arrested immediately and punished. He suggested that other Navajos wanted to make an example of them so there wouldn't be any more trouble in the future. He also provided the names of four witnesses and said he would be pleased to accompany the renegades to Santa Fe to testify as soon as the Native Fair was over, the first week of October.

Two weeks later, he sent a copy of this letter to the U.S. commissioner of Indian Affairs, Cato Sells. He added that the Navajos were armed and would not submit to arrest. He also passed on a rumor that a couple of them had been guilty of stealing horses. The commissioner was concerned enough to wire Shelton for more information. Shelton responded that warrants for the arrest of 12 men had been received, and two had already surrendered. The other 10 threatened to fight, and he doubted they would surrender without force. He requested that a U.S. marshal be sent to arrest them. Hatali Yazhe and his group were encamped on Beautiful Mountain with no intention of coming down.

On October 15, Commissioner Sells wired that he had requested the U.S. marshal to be called in. Once the federal government was involved, this local family matter became a matter of national concern.

At Sanostee, the bullpen became a place for people to gather and discuss what was going on and speculate about what would happen next.

Shelton sent Joe Tanner, an interpreter, to all of the local trading posts and businesses where white men could be expected to be found. Everyone was encouraged to leave their homes and businesses and go to the compound in Shiprock for their protection. One report even stated that Frank's life and the lives of other traders were individually threatened.

Rumors grew that some of the traders and their families were slated for death. Charley Nelson at Nava, about 35 miles south of Shiprock, Frank Noel at Sanostee, and OC Walker at Red Rock were among them. (9, pg. 94)

Most of them fled to safety.

Bizhoshi asked the Noels to stay. *Bizhóshí came to the store and told Noel not to send his wife and family away because a man needed a wife around, and that Little Singer was not angry at him and his family anyways. In my opinion, Noel, with his innate modesty and personal courage, tried hard to minimize the danger.* (9, pg.100)

In a later report, Shelton would explain that he had asked Frank and a few others to stay so it wouldn't arouse suspicion among the Navajos.

Frank remembers it very differently. He *had* been encouraged to leave, just like everyone else; but Frank and Mae decided they and their eight children would stay. Hatali Yazhe had been a friend, and they agreed to trust him. They stayed.

Noel family at Sanostee during uprising Source: 80 Years in America

Joe Tanner remembered it very differently too. In a later report he said, *That damned Frank [Noel] wouldn't budge, said he knew his Indians and I guess he does. They like him and he is good to them. But if he had heard what I heard, he would not be so sure of his safety.* (4, pg. 96)

Tension was mounting.

In a message sent to Shelton, Frank reported, *The Links [referring to Bizhoshi and his sons] are expecting trouble any day and are living at a high tension and the least thing may cause trouble to start here at any time. Several Indians have offered to come here and stay, so I do not think there will be the least danger in us staying here.*

The more the matter is talked over, the madder they get, and they have never changed an inch of what they first said, that if you wanted them you would have to come and get them. One of the gang comes down every day and sits around all day to learn if there is any news.

The Links have told around that if trouble started, they would take any good horses they happened to run on to. For that reason, some of the other Indians have armed themselves to protect their property. There will likely be something happen to start trouble soon if the Links are not taken care of. (10, pg. 354)

There was a sawmill nearby, run by another white man, Mr. Ayers. He and his family also decided to move to Sanostee until the trouble was over, rather than go to Shiprock. The Nelson family, Eliza Robinson (their current teacher), and Milton and Jennie Stelle were also staying. Twenty-three people were putting their trust in each other and their Navajo friends. Twenty-three people stayed.

Noel family and friends who stayed at Sanostee Source: 80 Years in America

Frank and Joe Tanner made a trip out to the Navajo camp to talk with the tribe about what they were hearing. Then Tanner went back to Shiprock, and they didn't see him again until the trouble was over.

On October 18, one month after Hatali Yazhe freed his wives from Superintendent Shelton's custody, Superintendent Paquette of Fort Defiance, just across the Arizona border, met with a Franciscan friar, Father Anselm Weber, from a local mission. He was the same missionary who had written to General Scott, years before, that Superintendent Shelton was not a good match for the job. Father Weber was well-known and respected in the area for his love of the Navajo people and his ability to help navigate difficult situations. Chee Dodge, a Navajo interpreter, peacemaker, and head chief of the Navajos, met with them. *As a result of the conference at St. Michaels, Anselm Weber, Chee, Peshlakai, Charley Mitchell, and Black Horse, all headmen of esteem, sought out Hatali Yazhe and his followers at a great squaw dance held in the Lukachukai Mountains. Hatali's group agreed to meet at St. Michaels for a general talk on the matter, but they insistently refused to surrender; over and over they repeated the issue basic to their stand; they had only taken back the three women who belonged to their clan.* (10, pg. 182) They agreed to meet at St. Michael's on Saturday, October 25, and the following Sunday at Fort Defiance.

They never showed up.

> *On the 29th of October, Rosenkrans [field officer] wrote a two-page letter to the Commissioner of Indian Affairs expressing his opinion in a frank manner. He stated the Indians had not appeared because they had heard that both Shelton and Hudspeth [U.S. marshal] would be there. The Indians wanted to discuss the matter with Father Weber. He continued, I must make it a matter of record that... I question the propriety of the arrest of the three women. And he went on to say the Navajos were also at fault for the way they retrieved them. (7, pgs. 263-264)*

Four days later, the **Farmington Enterprise** published the first account of the story, and it was quickly picked up by other papers. Soon the newspapers were having a field day with sensational headlines like, *Indians at Shiprock Threaten Revolt*. The game of gossip had begun. Shelton wired that Bizhoshi was on his way to Shiprock to ask for a complete pardon from the commissioner. If no pardon was to be granted, Shelton believed, his safety would be in jeopardy. Shelton then asked that he be permitted to employ sufficient force to hold the situation. The **Albuquerque Morning Journal** picked up that report and featured it as *Navajos threaten Raid on Shiprock Indian Agency*, which quickly became, *San Juan farmers sound the call to arms against hostile Indians*. And clear across the nation, a Washington, D.C. newspaper, in a dispatch dated Albuquerque, November 7, wrote of *threatened massacre of the entire agency* and stated that there had already been *raids against settlers, some homes had been burned, pillaging had taken place with stock being driven off, and white women and children abused.* (7)

Absolutely none of it was true. But people in Washington, D.C. didn't know that. The standoff became a topic of daily conversation. Hysteria was sweeping across the nation.

Fear was mounting on the Native side as well. They knew the troops were coming, and the lies being told about them could quickly result in an escalation of force. Was the whole clan in danger? What about the renegades? They had vowed to fight to the end. If things escalated, would that include killing traders and burning down their stores? They relied on the traders and worried about their safety. Some of them had become friends. They began to gather at various trading posts to find out what was going on.

Rumors spread locally, too. The Navajos heard that their women had been mistreated and abused while in custody. Anger grew. Determination not to give in grew. Hatali Yazhe began to worry he might not survive the confrontation that was coming. So he made provisions for his wives.

Late one evening, Little Singer came by the post [at Red Rock], *sending word to Walker* [the trader] *to come outdoors, to one side; he wanted to talk to him. Walker met him at the spot, but there were no other Navajos around. Little Singer told him that he wanted the trader to hold his pawn and that if anything happened to him, his wives should receive it. This pawn consisted of a valuable silver concho belt studded with expensive turquoise; coral, white shell, and silver beads; turquoise-mounted bracelets, rings, etc. He told him that he had heard what had been happening to the women since taken into custody. Walker replied that he did not believe those stories and that the agency authorities could not allow such things while the women were in their charge. There was, however, talk of troops being called out because his party had refused to surrender. The trader ended the interview by telling Little Singer that it was much better for him and his family to surrender on their own accord so that the authorities would not be too severe with him. The Navajo said he would think it over.* (5, pg. 97)

The Navajos at Red Rock had decided to encircle the trading post as they slept. Women, children, and older men slept in the center. Younger men slept on the outside keeping watch, guarding the large stacks of wood that renegades could use to burn down the store, preparing to spring into action if the need arose.

At the same time, Father Anselm Weber did his best to circumvent the lies by sending dispatches to government officials with the truth. However, his voice was drowned out by the half-truths circulating within and by the government and the newspapers wanting to capture the attention of their readers. There were even rumors that the life of Father Weber was in danger. It never was.

It must have been a constant topic of conversation at Sanostee. School for the children went on as usual. Customers came and went at the store, shelves were restocked, meals prepared, water carried, and wood chopped. But even the children had to feel something in the air as more and more Natives than usual camped around the store and riders shot back and forth between the trading posts. Everyone was trying to remain calm as they waited to hear what would happen next.

Chee Dodge, the head chief of the Navajo people, had been notified by the War Department to meet with General Scott at Sanostee to decide how to proceed. Father Weber learned that troops were arriving at Gallup from Nebraska and that General Scott would be leading them into Navajo country. Superintendent Paquette, Chee Dodge, Dr. Norbett Gottbrath, and Father Weber hurried to Gallup to meet with the general as soon as he set up quarters at the hotel. They needed to impress on him that many reports had been blown out of proportion, and he could settle the situation without hundreds of troops.

The general assured them that he had no intention of causing a bloody war. His plan was to show a large force in hopes of intimidating the Navajos into purposeful dialog. He recommended that Father Weber and Chee Dodge contact Bizhoshi and ask for a peaceful discussion at Sanostee in three days.

In Gallup… the four troops of cavalry from Fort Robinson arrived on two special trains Sunday night, November 23.… Considering that their adversaries now numbered twelve men, it was a strong force: 261 men and officers, supplied with 300 rounds of ammunition per man, 256 horses, 40 mules, and 8 wagons. (10, pg. 355)

The soldiers were camped about 20 miles from Sanostee, closer to Frank's other store, and they were understandably nervous. They had heard horrifying stories of what the Navajos might do to them. They built their fires as close to the store as they could.

The weather was horrible. The combination of snow and rain made the roads almost impassable. To make matters worse, when General Scott was on his way to Sanostee, he ran into Superintendent Shelton. Shelton urged an immediate assault on Beautiful Mountain before anyone could escape. The general had other ideas. He forbade Shelton from going anywhere near Beautiful Mountain until they were finished with their negotiations.

Shelton was not pleased but he did understand authority. Frustrated, he stayed away.

When Father Weber, Chee Dodge, and their party arrived, General Scott was already there. He told Frank he would let the Natives decide how to proceed. Runners were sent on to the camp at Beautiful Mountain to request that Bizhoshi come to another meeting with General Scott, Father Weber, and the Navajo leaders. Knowing Bizhoshi's love for family, and wanting to stress that the meeting would be peaceful, Father Weber also asked the runner to say that he should bring his young wife. It worked. The chief and his wife bravely made their way to Sanostee for the meeting.

Bizhoshi and General Scott met at Sanostee for one hour a day for three days.

November 26—*General Scott asked that the Indians be given food and allowed to eat and talk in the hogan supplied by the trading post for visiting*

Indians before they came into the council. The first day General Scott simply greeted Chief Bizhoshi and told him they had come to have a conference, and that he wanted him to go home and talk with his people and decide just what they wanted to say to him the next day; but that he and the soldiers had come a long way to help make peace between the Indians and the Government. (4, pg. 30)

Thanksgiving Day – A mutton feast was prepared in the hogan for the Navajos to enjoy before the meeting on the second day. Bizhoshi, his wife and daughters, along with the Navajo leaders, were all there. Once fed, the men went into the trading post to discuss what they would do. General Scott asked the Navajos to state their case first. They were outraged that their women had been taken and detained. They didn't want any trouble. They simply took back the women who belonged to their clan.

Then General Scott explained that some of their clan had broken the law by storming the stockade to take back their women. All people had to live by the laws of the land, whether they were white or Indian. The soldiers' job was to enforce those laws. He presented two options. Soldiers could be used to protect those who had broken the law as they peacefully escorted them to Gallup for trial, or they could go up on the mountain and forcibly bring out the renegades. If that were to happen, General Scott could not guarantee that the only people who got hurt would be the guilty parties. From a distance, it would be hard to tell who they were shooting at. They might not even be able to tell the men from the women. If, on the other hand, the guilty parties would surrender to him, they could go to court, serve their sentences, and return to live peacefully with their families.

Again, he asked them to go home and talk it over and return the next day with a decision.

*General Scott Source: **80 Years in America***

November 28—Tensions were high. Eighteen to 20 Indian men were packed in the bullpen area, anxious to hear how things would turn out. General Scott, in full uniform, sat with his back to the counter, facing the bullpen. His son, Lieutenant Scott, and Chee Dodge, acting as interpreter, were on one side of him. Frank sat on the other side. None of the men inside were armed, with the exception of Lieutenant Scott, who did have his revolver within reach in case he needed to defend his father. Mae and the other families sat in the living room with the children, just beyond the door of the bullpen where the men were talking. It's not hard to imagine them quietly praying for a peaceful outcome as they tried to keep the children quiet and hear what was being said. Seventy-five to 100 Navajos stood or sat outside the trading post. Many had come to offer themselves as substitutes if the accused men did not come down from the mountain. They wanted no trouble.

General Scott asked them what they wanted to do. Chee Dodge, who was greatly respected by the Navajo people, convinced the men to surrender. One by one, they came and asked for peace. When they were done, Bizhoshi got up to speak. He said that, if it were him, he would never surrender. Shaking with emotion, he said that he had never been afraid of the white soldiers, and he wasn't now. However, he was no longer a young man, and, if his son and the other young men wanted to surrender, he would concede.

He stepped outside with General Scott, and they shook hands, signifying to those waiting outside that the matter had been settled peacefully. Cheers went up all around, and they congratulated all involved for a job well done.

All of those waiting inside felt the weight of the past two months evaporate and said a quick but earnest prayer of thanks.

The terms of the surrender were generous. Two of the accused had not come down from the mountain. They had been out hunting and didn't get the word. General Scott gave the Navajos two days to go back, get their affairs in order, and bring the other two men with them. He waited at the store until they came down. Chee Dodge and Father Weber agreed to accompany the accused to Santa Fe for the trial, and prepared to leave with them.

There was a news blackout during the negotiations. But now, since the issue was settled, the newspapers were free to tell the story, or some version they thought would sell more papers. One reported that the renegades had surrendered to Shelton (which they never would have done). Another said Scott rode up to Beautiful Mountain to negotiate with them. He never had to do that.

On Monday, December 1, the accused, along with Father Weber and Chee Dodge, began their trek toward Gallup, where the prisoners would be put on a train headed for Santa Fe.

Their trial was held on December 3, just two days later. A court-appointed attorney for the accused argued that there was still a lack of understanding between the Navajos and the laws which they now needed to live under. He also emphasized that the case had been badly blown out of proportion and that the real threat was not nearly as bad as they had been led to believe.

On December 4, the courtroom was full of anxious locals wanting to hear exactly what was going to happen. They had come to believe these Natives were dangerous men, and now they were right in the middle of their town. They wanted to be sure the townspeople were going to be safe.

Bizhoshi and Hatali Yazhe were given 30 days in jail. Five men were given 10 days in jail, and one was set free. Their sentence was to be carried out at the Gallup jail so they could be near their families. The men were convicted, but grateful, and thanked the judge.

The sentences were carried out quickly and without incident.

A month or so after Bizhoshi and Hatali Yazhe returned from jail, General Scott met them once again at Sanostee. There were papers to sign. Frank never found out what they were for, or, he says, by the time he wrote out his story, he had forgotten. What he does include is that General Scott met Bizhoshi as an equal. They spent several hours, and, together with an Arapaho interpreter, talked about the origins of the tribe and some of the tribal beliefs and traditions. General Scott listened with real interest and, when he left, they parted as brothers.

CHAPTER 19:

Aftermath

The Beautiful Mountain rebellion and its aftermath had little effect upon the marriage of Little Singer and his wives. Most of the white traders thought the situation could have been handled differently, and they all agreed it was too difficult to end a custom that had been practiced for centuries. Education, not force, was the better remedy.

Little Singer lived a long life with two of his wives dying before him. He passed away peacefully, without bloodshed, and his body with personal possessions- belt, beads, bracelets, and rings – were placed in a rock cranny. (5, pg. 103)

It should be mentioned, too, that the fear generated across the country was slow to dissipate. The flames of mistrust, once fanned, were hard to cool down. Settlers in the area requested more protection and asked for an abandoned fort to be reopened. It was not.

Superintendent Shelton thought the sentences were a joke, and he never forgave Frank for staying and not running away. While there was talk about war all over the Shiprock agency, there was none at Sanostee. Frank and Mae's decision to stay made Shelton's reports seem exaggerated, not grounded in fact, and it cost him considerable credibility.

Shelton repaid Frank's bravery by giving a man a license for another trading post within three miles of Sanostee. Business gradually fell off. But the Noels had earned the love and respect of people all around the region. So, they were able to hang on… for a while.

CHAPTER 20:

A Gun, a Move, and New Schools

After months of tension, the summer after the "war" brought a welcome peace. The eight Noel children continued to grow and take an interest in the animals. When it was time to milk the goats, Frank held out his index finger and little Howard would grab onto it and go with him and brother Wright to the barn. Howard held onto the goat while Wright pushed with all of his might to keep the goat in place.

They still had their Sunday school, their walks in the desert, and afternoon picnics. Sometimes Frank was gone several days at a time when he needed to make a supply run. On those days, he hired someone to stay with Mae and the children and to help out with the store.

At the same time, Jennie had fallen in love with the sheep. She caught a ewe and held it still while an orphaned lamb nursed. This went on for quite a while until, one day, she tripped and fell back against the gate, and the ewe jumped over her head and out to freedom. The entire herd followed, leaving Jennie bruised and muddied in their wake. That was the last time she held a sheep to nurse!

Two very different things made the summer of 1914 one the family never forgot.

On August 11, 1914, Dr. Sammons rushed Mae to the hospital, and a sweet little girl was born. Frank came for a short visit and named their new daughter Virginia, after the beloved state where he was raised. Virginia was healthy and strong and a delight to the family.

Also, that summer, Mae had to take two of the children to the doctor at Shiprock, 30 miles away. She loaded Jennie, Howard, Mary, and Baby Virginia into the wagon while her sister-in-law, Eva, stayed with the rest of the children. Arriving in Shiprock about noon, they stopped for lunch, then headed on to the doctor. Howard, who needed his finger treated, was first to be examined. Then Jennie watched him and the baby while seven-year-old Mary had her turn. Mary's eyes really need treating. But little Mary, normally so sweet and compliant, wasn't having any of it. She pouted. She cried. She called for her father. She kicked and screamed. She ended up being held down so the doctor could treat her eyes. By the time it was over, Mae was exhausted.

But there was more trouble waiting for her.

Back at Sanostee, five-year-old Floyd, seeing his chance while his mother was away, climbed up on a high shelf and took down his father's automatic pistol to see the bullets. Overcome with curiosity, he reasoned that, if he pulled the trigger, the bullets would come up where he could see them. So Floyd looked down the barrel of the gun and pulled the trigger. There was a loud bang and Floyd fell screaming to the floor. The gun lurched, so the bullet went just above the collar bone and extremely close to the jugular vein. Two strangers heard the blast and rushed in to see what had happened. They bandaged the wound and insisted Eva get Floyd to the doctor immediately. A Navajo man agreed to rush them to Shiprock.

On their way, they passed Mae and the other children making their return trip. They stopped only long enough to tell them what had happened, then hurried on. Mae's heart sank. She was terrified for her son and wanted desperately to go with them, to do everything in her power to comfort him and make sure he would be okay.

But it was already getting dark. Mae was only 15 miles from home, exhausted, with a hungry baby whose bottle was missing, and three other exhausted children. What could she do that Eva wasn't already doing? She told Floyd to do exactly what Aunt Eva and the doctor said, and she continued on her way, worried about her son, and praying for his safety.

When she got home, tired and fearful, the other children were nowhere to be found! They weren't in the yard or the living room or the kitchen. She didn't know what could have happened to them all. She called out, but there was no answer. Now what?

Clara, now 13, who had been left in charge, was frightened by the strangers who jumped in when they heard the gunshot. She herded all of the children into one room and piled all of the furniture against the door so they would be safe. No one could come in. Then they just waited and tried to stay quiet until their mother got home.

When Mae finally found her children, fed the baby, put the other children to bed, and moved the furniture back in its place, morning wasn't far away. But Mae couldn't sleep thinking about Floyd, wondering how he was doing. She knew only too well that Floyd's life was not guaranteed. She had already lost one son. Exhausted, she fell to her knees and asked God to protect her little boy. He knew what Floyd needed. She believed that He loved Floyd as much or more than she did. When she finally felt God's peace, she drifted off to sleep.

It wasn't until the following afternoon that Eva drove in with Floyd. The doctor had dressed the wound, given instructions for his care, and sent them home. He was going to be all right.

Mae exhaled slowly and carefully hugged her son.

New Schools

At the end of the summer, it was time to again decide what to do about school for the children. So Frank rented a house in Farmington, New Mexico, directly across the street from a Catholic church and school. After talking with the three priests who lived there, it was decided that Reginald and Mary would attend the Catholic school, Clara and Jennie would go to the public school, and the five younger children would be home with Mae.

Since Frank had to go back to Sanostee, Mae was left, once again, to raise the children on her own. After a while, Mary, Mae's mother, came to live with them and help out with the children. They loved spending time together, and Mary was no stranger to a house full of children.

The priests and nuns at the Catholic church proved to be good neighbors. The Noel family was often invited to join their services and celebrations, and Mae found their Easter services very interesting.

With Frank coming and going, some of the children decided they could take on more responsibilities. Clara, 14, was determined to take over milking the cow. Reginald, now 10, managed many of the business dealings. He bought hay, coal, and whatever else was needed. Mae, for her part, seldom left home. She was often sick now with hay fever and asthma.

However, she did arrange for the other Mormons in Farmington to start meeting together, weekly, at her home. At the same time, the Noel children began to visit other churches with their friends from school. Like the Catholic church, they visited Methodist, Episcopalian, Christian Scientist, and Pentecostal congregations, taking note of what was foreign and what was familiar compared with their own religious practices.

One day in January, Mae received a message from Frank, asking her to meet him in Gallup on February first. From there they would go with friends, Bert and Sadie, to the World's Fair in San Diego!

Mae was excited but hesitant. It would mean leaving her mother, now 65, with the nine children and all of that housework. She knew how exhausting that could be. But her mother insisted. Frank insisted. And Mae's brother, Lou, volunteered to stay with Mary and the children. So it was settled. The adventure of a lifetime was about to begin!

It got a slow start.

CHAPTER 21:

Marvelous Adventure

Mae didn't start out until February 19th, and the first few days were spent trying to get to Gallup and Frank. Their friends, Bert and Sadie, had changed their minds about going, which meant Mae had to find another way. A friend agreed to take her as far as Sanostee, but the wagon got stuck in the mud. Finally free, they reached Sanostee, where Mae's brother, Frank Roberts, was tending the store. The next day, he took her as far as Toadlena, near Two Grey Hills, where they hired a wagon to take her on to Gallup.

Just as they were preparing to leave for Gallup, who should come up over the hill but Bert and Sadie! Having changed their minds again, they traveled all night to catch up. And they brought a surprise with them. More friends, George and Lucy Bloomfield, were coming too! It looked like it was going to be a real party!

Lucy was expecting a baby, so George hired a car and driver for them so she wouldn't be jostled around too much in the wagon and, hopefully, they could get there much faster. They set out. Unfortunately, the rain and the unpaved roads meant more mud. As the wagon Mae was riding in came over a ridge, she saw George and Lucy's car waiting for them up ahead. It, too, needed to be pulled out of the mud. This delayed them a bit, but there was lots of laughter and good-hearted jokes about a car that couldn't go anywhere. The third time it happened that day, it wasn't so funny.

When they finally reached Gallup the evening of February 23rd, Frank was waiting for them. They got hotel rooms and decided to see the town. Over the next day and a half, there were moments when the friends felt out of place in the faster pace of life in the city. But it certainly didn't stop them from shopping, going to a movie, and trying out a restaurant or two. It was already an adventure, and they weren't even out of Gallup yet!

When it was time to get on the train for California, the agent wished them well and suggested they look for the Baltimore Hotel when they got to Los Angeles. He also told them to wire him if they ran out of money.

The two-day train ride was itself an unexpected part of the adventure. Whizzing passed "worlds of cattle and sheep," mountains of lumber, saguaro cacti at sunrise, and a tribe of Zuni Natives kept them glued to the windows, afraid to miss a thing. The only downside was the short stops for meals along the way. This group was used to taking their time with food and not used to having to fight crowds to get to it. But the adjustment was worth it.

When they arrived in Los Angeles, they knew they were in a whole new world. They hailed a cab, checked in at the front desk of the Baltimore Hotel, and rode an elevator up to their rooms.

That afternoon, they went exploring. By the end of the day, they had seen the Soldiers' Home, watched as an orange slid down the throat of an ostrich, had their picture taken, eaten lobster for the first time, and were mesmerized by the peace and power of the Pacific Ocean. Most of them had never seen an ostrich, a lobster, or the Pacific Ocean before. So it was quite a memorable day!

The next couple of days were spent relaxing. They spent one day enjoying the beach so much that they missed their train going back. No problem.

They continued to swim, walk the beach, collect shells, and play on the slide and merry-to-round until the next train took them back to the hotel.

Mae's sister, Daphne, and her husband, Roy, lived in the Los Angeles area. When they went to see them, they were offered a room in their home for as long as they were in town. This became a base for Frank and Mae and gave them family time together. Some days were spent just exploring the beaches or planning what they would see at the World's Fair. One day ended up being primarily a sisters' day for Daphne and Mae. They decided to go to La Jolla and visit the grave of their father, Clark Roberts. Then, sitting on the beach, watching the waves, Daphne told Mae what their father's life in California had been like. It was a sweet time.

When they finally got to the World's Fair in San Fransisco, Roy made sure the Noels and their friends had access to the motorized chairs normally reserved for the wealthy. The fairgrounds were enormous and walking all day would really limit what they could see. Each state and territory had an exhibit. Some industries had additional exhibits promoting their latest technologies. Mae reports seeing a building filled with marvelous art—including landscapes, flowers, peacocks, exotic birds, and U.S. presidents—that had all been created by a Singer sewing machine! In other exhibits, they saw a sculpture of a girl milking a cow made entirely of butter, and an assembly line for coffee to "can itself." At the watchmaking exhibit, they saw screws so small that 2,250 of them fit nicely into a single thimble. They watched the processes for silk making, papermaking, and envelope making. They saw a crocodile weighing 2,300 pounds, a sea cow weighing 3,000 pounds, and humans weighing 500 pounds. They saw bamboo that was 45 feet tall, a giant redwood that was 300 feet in diameter, and a cheese weighing 1,500 pounds. They went to the largest park in the world, where they fed deer and saw huge bears, kangaroos, buffalo, ostriches, and all kinds of birds they had never even heard of. They watched a game of tennis for the first time, and saw mummies that dated back to 1000 B.C.

Source: palmsonthemove.blogspot.com/2015.04/miniature electric vehicles in 1915

The highlight for Mae was the "baby incubators." There was a room with glass walls, where they could watch nurses care for premature babies. Mae was amazed that babies born as much as three months early can be saved 85% of the time. To her it was an incredible sight. And later, it would give her real hope, knowing tiny babies had a good chance of survival.

The Tower of Jewels, the central building at the expo, was gorgeous at night with the light shining through it. Standing 433 feet tall, it dwarfed the other buildings around it. The friends found it to be an easy place to recognize and claim as a meeting place when they were separated.

Some of their vacation was spent on side trips in the area. A day at the shipyards instilled in Frank and Mae a new respect for the naval defense capabilities of the nation. There was a "flying boat" that went from ship to ship, and a lighthouse with cannons that were to guard the ships along the harbor. They also came to realize the immense contribution of the logging industry in building whatever people could dream up. Frank had worked in logging before, but he had never seen 900 feet of logs, bound with 250 tons of chain, floating along a river. They spent the rest of that day at the waterfront. Frank fished while the others were once again enchanted by the ocean waves and the beach. They even saw a sea lion and a shark!

Another day, Frank, Mae, George, and Lucy took a boat to Catalina Island. They were on the upper deck with lots of fresh air, but that didn't stop people around them from getting a little seasick. The first deck seemed to be full of people losing their last meal. Lucy and Mae were doing fine and wanted to see everything they could. Their ability to go below deck, where glass enclosures allowed them to see the workings of the ship and fish swimming over their heads, was thrilling. So they encouraged Frank and George to go with them on a later tour in a glass-bottom boat. Seeing the ocean floor itself, with its diversity of plants, fish, and other creatures, is something they could only imagine in the desert. It was spellbinding.

Back on shore, they met Daphne, Roy, Bert, and Sadie, and decided to go to the theater once more before calling it a day. After the theater, they ran to catch a streetcar, then had to take Daphne and Roy back to the train station. They were going home, but the friends were going back to San Fransisco. Saying good-bye to them was hard. They had enjoyed each other so much that week. It went by far too quickly. Who knew when they might see each other again?

The train ride back to Fresno was an interesting one. The countryside was so different from what they were used to, they found themselves just sitting and watching it go by. They climbed a mountain, going in and out of tunnels, catching glimpses of immense green pastures. There were fields of beautiful flowers, stockyards, orchards of every kind, and pretty little towns here and there that offered every kind of convenience imaginable. Mae was amazed at what man has the power to accomplish when he puts his mind to it. They stopped that night at the Collins Hotel and had the best chicken dinner they had ever eaten for a mere 25 cents (roughly $6.25 in today's dollars).

When they arrived in San Francisco, they were startled by the noise. The volume of traffic, people yelling and shoving, paper boys calling out the news, cabbies calling out the hotels they worked for, all seemed a little too much. It was hard to hear and harder to locate the bus they needed. When they found it, they started running toward it and hoped they wouldn't be left behind in the chaos. As it turned out, the driver saw them coming and graciously took their luggage to give them a moment to breathe.

Once settled into their hotel, they were determined to keep exploring. In Chinatown that night, they saw a man who could lift 336 pounds and a tightrope walker.

At Golden Gate Park, the next day, they saw buffalo for the first time. They also saw elk and bears, ducks, and about 20 seals sunning themselves on a huge rock. They walked through monuments of past presidents and famous poets, and marveled at the two Dutch windmills that were used to irrigate the park. One was 110 feet from tip to tip; the other was 84 feet. They saw a lighthouse and the Cliff House, and had their pictures taken again.

When they started walking down the oceanside boulevard, they were struck by how beautiful everything was. They were able to see the exhibition grounds and the city on one side and the powerful Pacific Ocean on the other. Two views in one spot, so different from each other, so different from home. They stopped for a moment to breathe it in.

All her life, Mae had heard about the giant redwoods in California from her father. So, she and Frank decided to see them while they were in the area. They boarded a train to see the giant trees, but were informed on the way that they had been told to board the wrong train. The conductor told them they would not be disappointed by the trip to the mountain, and they weren't. It was disappointing not to see the redwoods. But they had a chance to look through a telescope and have a good meal. It was all part of the adventure.

The Noels also wanted to see the Grand Canyon, but the others were ready for a day to rest. So Frank and Mae started out a day ahead of the others. They knew it was their last big side trip, and that was okay. They were both eager to be heading home, and at the same time a little reluctant to be leaving the lush land of California behind. But they did have time for one last adventure, and they were going to make the most of it. They slept that night sitting up in the train, and reached the Grand Canyon in time to eat breakfast at 7:30 the next morning.

They missed the burro ride to the bottom of the canyon, but were very satisfied to spend the day walking around its rim. The Grand Canyon is one of the seven natural wonders of the whole world! They ate a picnic lunch at Point Hopi, climbed the tower, registered their names, walked through the shops, and were really glad they had decided to take this side trip. There is one kind of excitement in going through exhibits and seeing so many unfamiliar and man-made things. But there is another kind of excitement that is bathed in the real peace that comes from just quietly sitting and looking at the natural wonders God has provided. The Grand Canyon is certainly one of those.

Back with friends, they spent the day riding the train back to Gallup and the little hotel they stayed in on their way west. For some reason, it didn't seem quite so grand this time around. The rooms looked smaller and shabbier than they had before. The good thing was, though, it meant they were closer to home. They were grateful for the trip and the mother and brother who had encouraged Mae to leave their nine children and go. They had had a wonderful time and learned a lot. But they both felt that it was time to head home.

That night, Frank received a telegram telling him his uncle, Frank Hambleton—his mother's brother, and the man he was named for—had died. He was to come to Baltimore, Maryland, immediately for the reading of the will. He left the next morning.

CHAPTER 22:

An Anxious Year

When Frank returned from Baltimore, he and Mae talked about what kind of education they wanted for the children. The children were growing up fast and, before long, their opportunity for an excellent education would be gone.

They sold the house and bought another house in Kirtland, just a mile from Fruitland. Frank donated an acre of land there to build a new school, so the children could be educated *and* close to the family. The school board had it up and running by the next school year. Frank was elected to the district school board, and he worked hard to encourage the community to come together and one day build a high school as well, so their children could be educated without having to move away from home. Mae became the president of the primary at church, and a brand-new life began for the Noel family.

When Dorothy was born on February 9, 1916, she was a delight to the whole family. But at two months, she had a spasm that scared them. Then she started losing weight. The doctor encouraged them to find a wet nurse, which they did. But despite being fed every 2 ½ hours, little Dorothy continued to lose weight.

All through the summer, they anxiously weighed her every day, hoping for improvement. She never got above three pounds and, at nine months, she weighed less than she had at birth. They were horribly afraid they were going to lose her and put out a plea for help.

When their friend, Cyril Collyer, arrived, they knelt and prayed together for wisdom about just what to do. They decided to take Dorothy to the doctor in Durango, 60 miles away. Leaving Baby Virginia with Mae's mother, and the other children with 15-year-old Clara and a friend, they headed out.

When they arrived in Durango, it was night and the doctors' offices were closed, so they had to wait anxiously until morning. When morning brought the doctor, he was faced with a nine-month-old baby who weighed only three pounds and parents who were terrified they would lose her. He didn't say much. He just gave some instructions to the nursing staff and left. Another anxious night. The following morning, when the doctor came by, Dorothy opened her eyes and smiled. The change in the doctor's face told them all they needed to know. There was hope. They still had a long way to go, but there was hope. Dorothy started to gain weight.

Frank eventually left to care for the other children and Mae stayed on at the hospital, eagerly watching for improvements. The day came when she had to leave the hospital but needed to remain close enough for the doctor to monitor Dorothy's progress. She says finding a place would have been easier if she had had a puppy instead of a baby. No one wanted a sick and crying baby in their building... even though this baby didn't really have the energy to cry at first.

When the crying did start one night, there was a predictable chain reaction. The man in the next room couldn't stand to hear it. He slammed the door as he stormed out. The landlady, not wanting to lose any more customers, told Mae that she and the baby had to leave. What could they do? Where could they go? When Mae told the doctor about it, he said Dorothy had recovered enough for them to go home.

Home sounded better than good. She called Frank and got them on the next train. Back in familiar surroundings, Dorothy gradually recovered and eventually thrived.

About that time, Mae's brother, Frank Roberts, contacted them with news of a land of milk and honey in Uintah County, Utah. It had good schools, good farming, good livestock, and a good church. Frank should come out and look for himself. He did.

CHAPTER 23:

Little Kingdom

The following February 1st, 1917, little Frank Roberts Noel, was born. He was named for both parents, taking his middle name from Mae's family; and, as all of the children had been, he was immediately considered a blessing from God. He is my father.

Frank looked at his new son and said, "Mother, I must get a farm so that these lads can grow up fine and big if we want them to make real American men."

It's just possible that having a family of 11 children was also a great motivator to find a bigger place.

The Algert Company, which supplied Sanostee, didn't want Frank to leave. They offered him a promotion and a raise if he stayed. But he dreamed of raising his family in a place not too different from Paynefield, where he grew up. The place he was looking for would be big enough for livestock, farming, and plenty of trees. It would be near good schools, good churches, and community events.

He found the perfect place in Vernal, Utah. The ranch was 280 acres, near mountain foothills for respite from the heat of summer, and had a creek for a constant supply of water. The schools and churches had good reputations and the town wasn't too far away. It seemed ideal.

Preparations for moving included selling Sanostee, selling the household goods they couldn't take, buying a car, and taking enough driving lessons to feel confident behind the wheel.

Their friends threw them a farewell party, complete with songs and speeches, at the little schoolhouse that had been built on their land. Saying good-bye to the life they built was hard. Saying good-bye to the Collyer family, who had been close friends for years, was even harder. But they were determined to make a new life for their family.

Curious about where Frank was going to end up, his brother Hambleton and a friend volunteered to go with them and help with the move. They set out in early April with two cars, five adults (including the driver of the second car) and 11 children, two of them on bottles. The youngest, little Frank, was only two months old. The wagons with the household goods had gone on ahead. The morning looked stormy, and most of the roads were not paved, so Mae suggested they start with a prayer. Frank said, "Well Mae, if you pray, I will work, and we will make it somehow." They expected the trip to take them three days. It took 12.

The first morning out, they felt like they were sailing along. By nightfall, though, it was snowing heavily. They found a little store with a family living in the back and, after some persuasion, talked the family into letting all 16 of them stay. By morning, there was a foot of snow on the ground, and it was still coming down. They had no choice but to stay until the roads cleared. Sixteen extra people was a lot for the family who lived there. They tried their best to make the Noel family comfortable. Mae had two bottle babies to care for. Clara and Jennie tried their best to help with the other children and whatever needed to be done. Nevertheless, over the next three or four days, they ate just about everything the little store had to offer, which took an unexpected chunk out of their travel money.

Once the snow stopped, the roads were soft. So Frank hired a team of horses to pull the cars out of the mud if they got stuck – the 1917 version of AAA Auto Service.

Places to spend the night along the way were few and far between. The ones they found were generally not expecting 16 people. At one place, the building was just one large room. The lady of the house pulled her own children to one side and encouraged Mae to take over the rest of the room and feed her family. Once the men were fed, they built a fire and slept around it outside, making room for the women and children inside.

When they stopped in Monticello, roughly 350 miles from Sanostee, it was snowing again. There was a hotel with plenty of room, and, as Frank started getting all of the children into the building, the owner told Frank it looked like he was a Mormon. Frank replied, "The better part of me is." They stayed there until the storm stopped, and headed out early while the ground was still frozen.

The next day was clear and warm, and they were in good spirits until that evening, when they came to a river that was running too fast and too high for the cars to cross. They were out in the country where there were no hotels or rooms to rent, and, when the sun went down, it was freezing. To top it off, little Virginia was running a fever. There was a cabin nearby, but no one was home. There was a sign on the door that warned trespassers against coming in. But Frank, believing they had no choice, unloaded the children, and asked Mae to start something for supper. Then he went to the field to find the owner and let him know what they had done. Mae was quite relieved to see them walking back to the house together. They could stay.

That night was spent with Mae tending the fire, covering the children who were sleeping on the floor with blankets or coats, and making sure Frank had a chance to sleep. After all, she reasoned, he had to drive the next day and so had their very lives in his hands. He should be rested.

By morning, the river had subsided enough to let them cross. So, they set out as early as they could. They had already lost a lot of time. During the day, they passed the two wagons they had sent on ahead with their household goods. Even with the delays, the cars were making better time.

At dusk, they came to the top of a hill where they were able to look down into Vernal, Utah, their new home. They were finally there. And just then, at the top of the hill, they ran out of gas.

A Real Home

In Vernal, they spent about a week in an empty house until they were finally able to move into their new home. Frank focused on the logistics of getting nine children to two schools, finding a church, and scoping out where they might have community dances. They really wanted to be able to go to dances again.

Mae describes it as her first "real home." It had four bedrooms, a kitchen, a pantry, a parlor, and a bathroom with a real bathtub. Until now, they had been bathing in a small round tub with pitchers of water poured over their heads. With a real bathtub, everyone was excited for bath time. The little ones could almost swim in it! The dining room was a bit small for their large family, but they would worry about that later. There were bay windows in the kitchen and parlor that Mae soon filled with flowers. There was an ice-house and a second building with two rooms they used for a storehouse. There was a large garden where they would grow enough vegetables to get them through the winter.

There was also a barn, and pens for calves, pigs, and chickens. There were bees and a bee house. There were fields of hay and grain. In short, their new home was exactly what they were looking for, and something that would require endless full, hard days of work.

They were delighted.

As Mae writes, Some call it hard work. It is hard work, but it is work that makes us healthy and happy. It is work that develops our boys and girls physically, mentally, and spiritually. It makes characters to be depended upon. It makes men and women who can think and act for themselves, men and women who, in turn, can face the trials of life with courage and happy hearts, who are ever ready to help others in trouble. And can fit in any corner they happen to be called to. That is what our children can do. Thank the Lord for the good, old ranch. (4, pg. 109)

Frank describes it this way. We raised a big crop of hay and grain, bought more cattle, and a number of milk cows, chickens, and hogs, and had a big garden. These things are vitally necessary when you attempt to raise a big family, which at this time numbered eleven children. We had a splendid life on the ranch. We owned saddle horses, wagon horses, and heavy draft horses. I had to have a hired man for the first few years, but as the boys got bigger, we were able to do our own work.... These were glorious times. The boys each had his own saddle horse, and I had mine. We ran cattle in Diamond Mountain and had a big pasture at home. Our table was set with thirteen seats. You have no idea the amount of bread, milk, butter, meat, and vegetables it takes to feed a family of eleven. As time went on two more came, making a family of thirteen children and two parents, so we had a table set with fifteen seats. For years this meant forty-five meals every day, and when the boys and I were working in the hay field, and irrigating the alfalfa, the meals had to be substantial and regular...We raised everything we used to a large extent, even our flour was from our own wheat, ground at the mill, and all vegetables and meat were raised on the ranch. In fact, we had a little kingdom of our own, and I repeat, those were glorious years. (4, pg. 33)

A typical day at the ranch for the children went something like this:

+ Up at 6.
+ Milk eight cows.
+ Feed the cows and horses.

- Eat breakfast.
- Participate in family prayer.
- Make beds.
- Girls pack 10 lunches. Boys harness horses and get buggies ready.
- Make beds.
- Wash up and gather things for school.
- Travel three miles there.
- Have school.
- Three miles home.
- More chores to do, including getting clothes ready for the next day.
- Supper.
- Homework from 7 to 9 around the table.
- Family home evening presentation.
- Games.
- Bed.

For the parents, there wasn't much downtime, either. As long as they were living there, there were children too young to go to school who needed tending. That included bottles to wash and diapers to change and wash. There was also cooking 45 meals each day from the things they grew on the ranch. That amounted to preparing, cooking, and washing up after about 16,425 meals a year. Housecleaning needed to be done, to some extent, daily. Laundry for 15 people was divided among the older girls. Once the clothes were washed, each of the older girls had responsibility for her own clothes and three of the little ones'. They would sort out the clothes they were responsible for, choose what was to be worn the next day, iron and mend those, and set them in a pile so they would be ready to dress the next day.

There was also the ranch to manage. That included:

- planting, caring for, and harvesting the huge garden
- care and feeding of horses, cows, pigs, chickens, and turkeys
- planning, planting, irrigating, and harvesting crops

- getting crops to mill or market
- maintaining buggies and buildings
- keeping track of finances

It is amazing what they expected themselves to accomplish on a daily basis.

In the summer, there were the crops to manage. Some years they had 100 tons of hay, not to mention wheat and barley. The cattle were taken up on the mountain for fresh grass. Also in the summer, Mae had terrible hay fever and would need to go up on the mountain for a month or so in June. She would take some of the children and some of the saddle horses, and they lived in a tent until Frank was able to build a little cabin on the cattle range. All the children learned to be expert riders. All learned to love the beautiful land that surrounded them.

Frank and Mae with 10 of their children on the mountain.
Source: 80 Years in America

In the fall, the cattle came down from the mountain. To feed them, large amounts of hay would be pitched from a sled, one boy on each side. On especially hot days, or lucky days, the girls would churn ice cream and take it out to the fields, and work would stop for a little while.

Eventually, friends and family became frequent visitors, and they loved the feeling of community that provided. Unfortunately, though, for the first few years, the whole world was turned on its ear and visitors were not possible.

Pandemic

While the Noel family was enjoying their little kingdom, the rest of the world was thrown into turmoil. In March of 1918, the first known case of the Spanish flu was documented in Kansas, USA. By April, cases had been documented in France, Germany, and the United Kingdom. It was near the end of World War I, and wartime censors were hesitant to talk about it for fear their enemy would see their country as vulnerable. Spain was not a combatant, so they were more willing to be honest about what was happening within their borders. As a result, many believed this virus originated in Spain instead of the U.S. Hence the name "Spanish flu." In reality, it was a variant of the H1N1 virus that caused the Russian flu and the swine flu later on.

By 1920, two years later, nearly one-third of the global population, or around 500 million people, had been infected. Estimates of fatalities range from 17 million to 100 million worldwide.

The schools closed, a mask mandate was put in place, and public gatherings were canceled. A teacher in the Ashley district, where my grandparents lived, took children one at a time and rehearsed the lessons for the week. Many students struggled, though. Focus and momentum are difficult when you are grieving a loved one.

As the world was reeling under the pandemic, the timing for the Noels to move to their little kingdom was ideal. Frank closed the front gate to the property and made sure no one came in or went out without his approval.

They were as close to being self-sufficient as they could be. Everything they truly needed was on the ranch. Being isolated was, for them, not a problem. As a matter of fact, it turned out to be a blessing. They missed their friends, but their priority was family.

One person who was allowed to come in was the new doctor. He was needed to help deliver their thirteenth child. Most of the doctors had been called to the war effort, so this new doctor was someone Mae had never met. Nevertheless, on November 10, 1919, Donald was born, a healthy boy, and the family rejoiced.

In town, and around the world, the virus was taking a fearful toll. Sadly, Villa Collyer, Mae's best and longest friend, was among the casualties.

No one at the ranch was infected. The only thing lost there was the Buick. It was no longer needed.

Return to Normal

When the children were finally able to return to school, so were the teachers. One summer, Mae's sister Daphne had to go back to school herself to keep her certification. What could she do with her own children while she was in school? Roy had left them, so she had no one to share that burden with. Naturally, her six children joined their Noel cousins, giving the Noel family 18 children, six of whom were under five years old. Clara and Jennie were already busy helping Mae with cooking, laundry, and gardening. So, Mary and Bessie were assigned to the six youngest children, taking over their care completely. A small table was set up on the lawn for their meals, Mary and Bessie managed their daytime activities, laundry, meals, and baths; and for six weeks they all lived as one family. Thankfully, they had the room. Daphne eventually returned, a bit rested, and qualified to teach again.

For the next few years, life rolled along quite nicely. Grandma Mary joined them in 1921 and took over the chickens and turkeys while they awaited the birth of their fourteenth and last child. On July 29, 1921, Roane Chadwick was born. He was named after one of his father's friends from childhood, and a character in a story that the children all loved. He was called Chad and was immediately loved by all the family.

Frank and Mae with their 13 living children, 1921. That cute 4-year-old
between his parents is my father.
Source: 80 Years in America

The hard work and full schedules listed earlier soon became the normal ebb and flow of the days. There were the animals to care for, the schoolwork to see to, and the never-ending meals to prepare. Mae baked nine loaves of bread three times a week. In the summer, they churned ice cream every day, with the younger children eager to turn the crank.

As the pandemic ended, Frank took on feeding a herd of white-faced heifers. He quickly fell in love with them and decided to buy the herd. It was quite an investment. The boys were elated and quickly found ways to make themselves helpful.

Shockingly, sometimes the children were late for school.

Okay, the children were often late for school. One year, Mary was told to write an essay on why she was late so often. At the same time, she was studying for exams and also chosen for the debate team. She didn't have any idea what to say. Mae encouraged her to just tell the truth. So she did. She told of milking cows, helping with breakfast, making lunches, washing dishes, participating in morning prayers, getting herself and younger siblings ready for school, and nagging her brothers to please hurry and get the horses and buggies ready. Evidently, she told it with a bit of humor, and the teacher loved it. He enjoyed showing the essay around to other teachers so much that he never gave it back. But Mary never got in trouble for being late again.

CHAPTER 24:

Growing Up

The children were growing up. Frank remembers Mary and Bessie winning debates against every school in the area. He remembers Reginald being the best in mathematics and Floyd excelling in basketball and track, while Wright and Howard added boxing and wrestling. He remembers Frank, Virginia, Dorothy, and Donald as being good students as well.

Clara and Jennie had both graduated from high school, starting a record of 13 children from the same family graduating from Vernal High School. But there is another part of the story.

While Frank remembers all the children being fine students, young Frank tells a slightly different version. He remembers getting into a bit of trouble in high school, nothing horrible, just hanging with the wrong crowd. His father sent him to work with the sheep and arranged for Dorothy, just a year older, to bring his assignments to him and take the finished ones back to school. Sometimes, if the papers were dirty from the fields, she would recopy them before she turned them in. Well, after a while, it seems that young Frank gave up and quit sending in assignments. But his faithful sister, unbeknownst to Frank or their parents, never quit turning them in. At the end of the school year, my father received an unexpected invitation to come to school for his final exams. What could he do?

He telephoned the headmaster and told him that he wasn't able to come in since he was working for his dad. Then he wondered out loud if the headmaster thought he would pass the tests if he could come in. The headmaster enthusiastically agreed. His grades had been excellent. In the end, the headmaster allowed Frank to graduate with his class, even though he missed most of his senior year, including his final exams. I still have his class ring.

When Clara graduated, she went on a mission to California. On April 27, 1922, Jennie married Otis Weeks. The children were starting to leave home. Most went on missions for the Latter-Day Saints church. But home and family were still very important to them.

Jennie continued to make the annual trip to the mountain with her mother during hay fever season. When they went, it felt like they were going to their own little mountain resort. They all looked forward to it. Sometimes they would bring friends along. Floyd once asked Mae when she was going to get hay fever again so they could go to the mountain. It never took long. After all, they did live in the middle of acres and acres of hay.

On the mountain, they sometimes put boards on the side of the wagon, loaded the children and picnic baskets inside, and took the meal wherever they wanted to explore. The children came back with loads of flowers, and the general feeling was one of peace and contentment.

Except for one year.

Frank and Otis, Jennie's husband, decided to take some time out to go on a fishing trip. They pitched tents in a grove of trees near a stream and got ready to go. Mary, Bessie, and a friend decided to go with them, leaving Jennie and her baby with Mae and the rest of the children. As he started to head out the next morning, Frank told Mae, "Sometimes the flies get bad up here. If they do this time, you will have to protect the children."

Protect the children from flies? Of course. How bad could it be?

As soon as the sun came up, she found out. The flies started swarming. They were swirling *everywhere*, and they were hungry. The horses strained against their reins trying to get closer to the smoke of the campfire. Mae called for the children to build more campfires and cover them with weeds to increase the smoke. The children and the horses tried standing in the smoke. The cows went crazy and ran away. She sent two children off on horseback to find them: one to guide the horse, and one to keep the flies away. No luck.

Sticking around the campsite was just not an option. They had to get out of there, even if it meant losing their cows.

Moving as quickly as they could, they took down the tent; packed the food, dishes, and blankets; loaded up the wagon; and headed down the hill. The only problem was that the wagon had a brake that would catch sometimes. Howard positioned himself so he could jump down on the brake when it was needed, then jump back up in the wagon. It was slow going over the rocks. Wright, Jennie, and her baby came behind in the buggy. It wasn't any faster for them.

Inch by inch, they made it to a place they recognized, and decided to stay. The flies were not so bad there, and they had only hay fever waiting for them if they went home. Mae didn't want to take a chance going down the rest of the hill with the brake the way it was. So they pitched a tent under some trees and waited.

The next day, a man came by who said he had seen their cows and kindly volunteered to go get them. He was an answer to prayer. Wright went with him, and brought their cows safely back to where they belonged.

Two days after that, the fishing party of Frank, Otis, and the girls caught up with them and seemed unsurprised that they had moved from the original campsite. There is no mention of whether they brought fish back with them or ate them all while they were away. There is no mention of how they found the new campsite. Mae does mention that she wonders if she or Jennie will ever completely forgive them for leaving them there, knowing how bad the flies could be. She obviously never forgot it. In the end, they just moved the campsite again to a beautiful little spot with no flies and a stream running by. It would become their permanent mountain spot until a cabin was built.

Christmas

The Christmas of 1922 stands out in Mae's memory, not because it was so unusual, but because it was the last one before Grandma Mary had her stroke and passed away. Everyone came for Christmas except Clara, who was on her mission. Those children who had gone out on their own came back with their families. Mae remembers her mother holding Baby Chad as 17 people marched around the Christmas tree, singing "Jolly Old St. Nicholas." Ronald Preece, who would later marry Clara, was dressed up like Santa and, every time they marched by his spot, Grandma Mary would have him shake hands with the baby. Just as the presents were distributed, Daphne came in with her six children and, as always, they were quickly incorporated into the fun.

Dishes of nuts, oranges, candies, and apples were placed all around so they could eat as much as they wanted. No one seemed interested in breakfast, but dinner was another story. Mae doesn't go into detail about what was served, only that tables were set up the length of the house and they were overflowing "with everything Christmas calls for."

There was lots of food and singing, and lots of dishes for the 24 of them. Ronald, Clara's boyfriend, stood washing at the sink for quite a while. The memory of that day brought a smile to Mae's face years later.

CHAPTER 25:

Kingdom's End

F ew things last forever.

The children kept growing and moving away. Frank remembers it this way: *Children grow into men and women, get married, leave home, and start their own families. In this case, there were thirteen children, and, one by one, they left home, took positions for themselves, got married, and began the wonderful job of there being thirteen families instead of one family. . .. And so our little kingdom began to disintegrate.* (4, pg. 36)

Life was changing.

In 1922, there were other predictable yet unexpected changes. Then, as now, the aftermath of the pandemic produced financial uncertainty in the general economy.

It wasn't long before the *worldwide* financial community was in turmoil. Economists will tell you there were several factors:

- A new international tax slowed down international commerce.

- A drought resulted in less hay and higher prices to feed livestock.

- An overabundance of optimism in goods and services led to plummeting prices as sellers jockeyed for position to sell what they had, quite often at a loss.

- There were poor banking practices on both the individual and federal levels. *In all, 9,000 banks failed--taking with them $7 billion in depositors' assets. And in the 1930s there was no such thing as deposit insurance--this was a New Deal reform. When a bank failed the depositors were simply left without a penny. The life savings of millions of Americans were wiped out by the bank failures.* (http://www.ssa.gov/history/bank.html.) Imagine hearing your bank has closed and your life savings have disappeared without a trace. Rumors, unverified, circulated about investors jumping out of windows to their death. Some people literally took to hiding their money under their mattresses, where they knew it would be safe.

- At the same time, those bankers who remained solvent sometimes charged high interest rates and then took personal property to pay off delinquent loans.

At the Noel ranch, as the Great Depression advanced, they were hit with all of it. To begin with, the cost of beef dropped significantly at the same time the price of feed went up. Frank sold the herd of white-faced cattle they had grown so fond of at a loss. With a loan from the bank, they decided to try sheep. Reginald came home and helped with the ranch for a year. When they sold the lambs in the fall, there was enough money to make a payment to the bank, but nothing left over for those who had worked all year raising the sheep. Frank, downhearted and embarrassed, encouraged Reginald to move on and find a different path. He did.

That same year, there was a cloudburst in the hills above the ranch. Water poured down on the fields below, covering them up to a foot deep. They came home from church one Sunday to find the alfalfa and wheat crops completely wiped out. Another unsettling loss.

The next year Frank reluctantly sold the ranch and moved the family to a much smaller location, only 10 to 12 acres compared to the 280 acres they had just sold. It had a good pasture and room for a nice garden. So they took a few horses and milk cows and they tried to start over. Dorothy, Frank, Donald, and Chad, their four youngest children, were still at home. They had to find a way to keep going.

They hauled coal and they tried to rent out the farm equipment they still had to farmers who were still working. But the farmers were operating at a loss already and couldn't pay. So, they lost the farm equipment, too.

Mae was not well. Hay fever, asthma, and rheumatism continued to plague her. Then she sprained her knee... and started a little kindergarten. She would meet the children in the morning as she hobbled along on crutches. They were doing everything they could think of to stay afloat.

More of the milk cows and some of the sheep were sold to finish paying off the last of the bank loan. Wright and Howard collected their parents and took them to a ranch in Brush Creek, about 800 miles away, where they were leasing a small herd of sheep. They could only take the parents. There wasn't room for the children too.

They arranged for Bessie, who was already working as a teacher, to take in the four youngest siblings. They turned the garage into sleeping quarters, but it was cold. Mae remembers seeing ice on the beds at times. It broke her heart. Still, they had to make it work and be grateful it wasn't worse.

Everyone tried to keep going as best they could. Floyd was sent on a mission with the church. Wright soon went to Agricultural College and Ronald, Clara's husband, took over his place with the sheep. Some of the older girls just took odd jobs here and there. Virginia was working her way through school by raising turkeys.

In March of 1933, Wright had to quit school because of finances and came home to take care of the sheep. It had been a horrible winter. Frank's records reminded him that it snowed every single day in February. Fully half of the sheep died. Wright leased another small herd and optimistically added them to the remnant of the first.

Floyd was home from his mission, but that summer he was appointed the fish and game warden for Uintah County. He would not be able to help with the sheep, but he would not have to worry about losing everything in this voracious depression. His parents were happy for him.

Wright continued to work for the company they were leasing the sheep from, and eventually had an opportunity to move out of state with them. At home, the future looked bleak. Frank was simply tired and discouraged. That fall, he threw in the towel. He returned the whole lease of sheep and land back to the Humphrey Phosphate Company, but that didn't cover their debt. In that settlement, he turned over everything he owned: their home, the last of the cows, even some of their furniture. They were left with the clothes on their backs.

He grieved the loss of the ranch. They had such happy memories there. But now, Mae, who had pushed so hard for years, even through her pain, needed help and rest. Her asthma and hay fever were getting worse. Frank would have loved to give her a season of rest. He needed it too, but it didn't look like it was going to happen for either of them anytime soon.

Frank also grieved that he couldn't put all the children through college. Only a few got to go. Wright only got two years. Some who were younger didn't go at all unless they found a way to pay for it themselves. He had hoped; he had *planned* to provide that for all of them. But he had nothing left.

He admits to being cranky. She admits to being tired. Both were discouraged. Snide comments and hours of not talking at all would have been understandable. Mae was still rooted in her faith. Her positive attitude helped, but Frank worried about starting over when they had nothing to start *with*. He knew how to be resilient. He prided himself on the ways he had found to bounce back in the past. But now, he was already in his 60s, the full life expectancy for a man living through the Depression. And he still had four children who were not yet grown.

The turning point came one day when Mae and Frank passed each other in the yard. They stopped and talked about everything that was happening. Then they agreed not to worry about finances anymore. They had come through a lot in their married life and were glad to still be together. They would focus on each other and the children. No stress. No pressure. No more dreams of getting ahead. Just live day to day for those they loved. They even shook hands on it. Somehow, with God's help, it would get better. It had to.

And it did… in a completely unexpected way.

CHAPTER 26:

Public Life

For some time now, Frank had been advocating for the Navajo people to get voting rights, and he was well-known for his work in that arena. His family was also well-known and admired for their work in the church and in the schools. The fact that he had been through the financial wringer meant that he was able to relate to many others who were struggling in the same way. So, despite the fact that he had lost everything and had to move in with his children, Frank was nominated for county clerk and auditor.

With plenty of time on his hands, he began to make a few short speeches around the county. Mr. Hyram Calder would introduce him as a man of few words. Then he would speak for about five minutes on how he would do his best to set things right and see the county solvent again. He was elected November 7, 1934. He took office two months later and served for the next 12 years.

What a change! Regular paychecks came without the back-breaking work that sometimes ended with no pay. They rented a home and brought the four youngest children back to live with them. They stayed there for three or four years and were then able to buy a home of their own.

For Mae, life was different, even if her focus was the same. For one thing, she had time to concentrate on her own health! Dorothy had just graduated from high school, and had her heart set on becoming a nurse. At the same time, the doctor saw that Mae had really worn herself completely out. She was in serious shape and would need a good stretch of time to rest. So, he promised Dorothy he would get her into a really good nursing program at a really good hospital if she would first take a year off and take care of her mother. She quickly agreed and made sure her mother followed the doctor's orders to a "t." Mae believed she had no choice but to do as she was told. After all, her daughter had put her dreams on hold for her. Instead of cooking 45 meals a day, tending a garden, washing clothes, and trying to keep up with the lives of 13 children, she rested. As a result, she got better. Mae credits Dorothy, and the time she dedicated to her, for actually saving her life.

At the end of the year, the doctor was true to his word and made a place for Dorothy to study nursing at a good hospital. But Dorothy's dreams had changed. Instead of becoming a nurse she married DeMar Gale and spent all her years being the best wife and mother she could be.

Other than that year of rest, Mae doesn't talk much about their new public life. Rested and healthy, she spent the next years, as she had the previous years, focused on her children, her husband, and her church.

For Frank, the work as county clerk was pleasant and he was good at it. As county clerk, he saw all of the legal challenges that were going on around him, and was partly responsible for keeping them on track. So, for example, if he saw a deadline approaching, he checked in with the parties involved to be sure they were ready. He also had a lot of influence in the financial dealings of the county, and this is where he felt the most useful. Over time, with the help of the treasurer, the assessor, and county commissioners, he instituted a pay-as-you-go policy for the county. Debts were paid and the county was once again on a solid financial footing after the devastation of the Great Depression.

Another benefit of being in county government was that it gave Frank an insight into and an appreciation for the United States that never left him.

In 1944, in addition to his other duties, Frank volunteered for the Department of Selective Service and received a letter of gratitude from President Harry S. Truman.

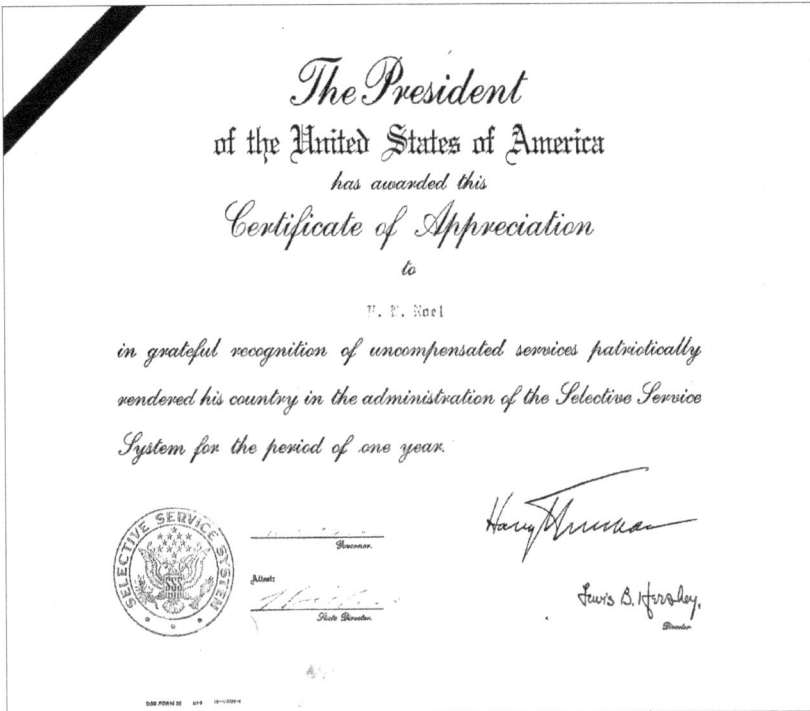

Letter from President Truman (2)

Each January, the officers in each of the 29 counties of Utah would meet in Salt Lake City for three days to go over state business. On the third night, there would be a banquet and a floor show for the officers, their wives, and friends. Normally, that meant about 500 people. The excitement of the conference was contagious, but, more importantly, Frank felt a part of something bigger than his small part in the local government. He was able to meet people and give opinions about things that would matter to all the citizens of Utah. It felt bigger and he was pleased to be a part of it.

In addition to state conferences, delegates from 3,000 U.S. counties met each year for a national conference. After the meetings, classes, and entertainment were completed, they chose a city to host the conference the following year. In that way, returning delegates got to visit different cities, and different cities took turns benefiting from the tourism generated by the conference.

In 1946, the commissioners from Uintah County asked three officers to go to the national conference in Cincinnati, Ohio. Roy Labrum, commissioner, Frank Noel, clerk, and Lester Bingham, assessor, were each given $175 to cover their expenses.

Decades later, Frank said it was the best trip of their lives. (4, pg. 42)

For one thing, their daughter Jennie and her husband Otis not only went with them, but decided to drive their own car. For another thing, they decided to keep going after the meeting in Cincinnati and go all the way to Washington, D.C. Visiting the nation's capital was a dream come true! The first night they made it as far as Denver. The second day they were in Kansas. They saw the state capitol in Topeka. But the thing that was really awe-inspiring in Kansas was the miles and miles of wheat fields. For the Noels, watching the giant combines cut, thrash, and stack 20 bushels of wheat with each pass was jaw-dropping. They remembered how much work it was to harvest hay in their little kingdom years ago. Learning how the farmers rotated the fields to maximize production was also fascinating. This truly was a different world.

Coming across sections of land where oil wells were pumping oil, day and night, without a single person in sight was another revelation. Here, business was running even when no one was there!

In the first three days, they had easily crossed an 11,000-foot mountain pass that would have been nearly impossible with horse and wagon, They had gone through the never-ending wheat fields, and then crossed the mighty

Mississippi River, vastly bigger than the San Juan River back home. Each of those things was a new and enlightening experience.

On the fourth day, they arrived at the national conference in Cincinnati. There were three days of meetings and classes. Frank was able to meet and share ideas with county officers from around the country. The hotel provided a wonderful floor show, and excursions were available during their downtime. Frank remembered a steamboat trip they took on the Ohio River. All in all, it was a very satisfying experience.

But the best part was still to come.

When the conference was over, they headed on to Washington, D.C.

There they visited all of the tourist spots. Knowing this was a once-in-a-lifetime experience, they didn't want to miss a thing. They saw the Capitol Building, the Washington Monument, the Jefferson Memorial, the Lincoln Memorial, and the Tomb of the Unknown Soldier at Arlington Cemetery. They sat in on a session of the Senate, and visited the Treasury Building, where they found out how money is made and how it is guarded. They were able to see the actual Constitution of the United States and how it was guarded as well. They went to the home of Robert E. Lee and then on to one of Frank's favorite memories, Mount Vernon. I will let him tell it in his own words.

> *Then we went on to the Great Shrine of all Americans, Mt. Vernon, and I sat in the same rocking chair that was used by George Washington and looked out on the same Potomac River that he loved. I was thrilled to go through Mt. Vernon. We saw the library, the big bed, which Washington used, and the old-style kitchen and buildings for the workers. I was thrilled to see the home life of our greatest American; for George Washington has always been that to me, and one of the great men of all time and all countries. (4, pg. 43)*

From there, Frank goes on to encourage anyone raising children to take them on a similar trip when they are old enough to appreciate it. He believed it couldn't help but fuel their respect for and dedication to the United States, "the finest land in all the world."

When they left Washington, D.C., they went to Baltimore, Maryland, where Clara, Frank's mother, was raised. They visited Greenmount Cemetery, where his father, mother, and young sister Bessie are buried.

From there they met a relative Jennie found through her genealogy work, Evelyn Noel Godman. Evelyn was very interested in the family genealogy, so she and Mae and Jenny had an immediate bond.

The next stop wasn't quite so pleasant. Paynefield—the plantation where Frank was raised, the plantation he thought of as home—was badly in need of repair. It had been 55 years since he stood here. Memories of riding his horse six miles to school every day, running with his brothers and his dog, cultivating his own piece of land, and spending time with his mother every day, came flooding back. He visited the cemetery in the back of the house, where his grandparents were laid to rest, and took a moment to look around. It was sad to see his old home so run down.

The Andrews family, who had bought the property decades earlier, still owned it. But the parents were no longer able to keep it up, and the sons had gone into the army. World War II, which had ended not long before, was devastating on many levels. He could understand how the decline happened. But it was still hard to see. (Read Chapter 28, "Then and Now," for a happier look at Paynefield today.)

In Tappahannock, in the square in front of the country house, there was a bronze statue in honor of the 52nd Regiment of the Virginia Cavalry. Frank found his father's name there: Dr. Henry R. Noel. He says that, when the statue was dedicated, his cousin Edmund F. Noel, governor of Mississippi, gave the dedication address.

The statue has since been removed, but the plaque that bears the name of Dr. Henry R. Noel, surgeon, is still there.

Source: Timothy Manley, Essex County Museum and Historical Society

The trip back home took them through Virginia, Tennessee, Arkansas, Oklahoma, and Colorado. In each state, they stopped to admire the capitol building and some of the major universities and businesses.

Ten days after they returned home, the primary election was held. Frank did not run for a fourth term. His hearing was going, and it was time to pass the baton. That November another man was elected county clerk, and January 7, 1947, weeks before his 74th birthday, Frank turned over the office.

US Congressman Don Colton with Frank Noel and their wives.
Source: Private Collection

That experience and his pride in our country never left him. Here is a letter he wrote in his final years to his descendants and sent to President Lyndon Johnson:

Dear Friends and Relations,

FIRST: I am in good health for a 92-year-old.

SECOND: I am intensely proud of all of you and accept you as you are today, no change of any kind asked for, and I have a place in my heart for each and every one of you.

My desire in life since 1898 has been to have a Home and Family that is a credit to me and to the country in which we live. I have succeeded in this desire more than my wildest dreams, and even now I am ignorant of the reason I was selected to start such a family. I am intensely proud and thankful for my position in being responsible for such a "Wonderful

Group." Then when providence calls, I will pass on, a proud father and a contented citizen of America.

SOME OF MY THOUGHTS:

We read in the papers of the claim that some individuals want to clear up the mess in Washington. There is no mess, only in their own minds. It is good for any country to have more than one party. Each party stimulates all the others to better efforts for Peace, Liberty, and Advancement.

What they really found in Washington was the finest, strongest, and best government in all the world. At present it is the hope and trust of the civilized world. A government that does not conquer other nations but frees them and helps them Stay Free.

At the present time the greatest honor in all the world is to be an AMERICAN CITIZEN. In my language the big word is Friendship, not Money

I ask that this letter be shown to all the two hundred of our Noel Family.

Your friend,
Frank L. Noel (4)

CHAPTER 27:

Retirement and Beyond

The month Frank retired, they sold their home in Vernal and bought one in Draper, "where the snow does not get so deep and zero (degrees) is unusual." Both conditions were better for Mae's health and were a practical step in the right direction for a couple in their 70s. Life was changing; the culture was changing. But Frank and Mae Noel had vowed to live each day as it came. So they approached the changes calmly and handled each one as it happened.

Draper, less than 20 miles from Salt Lake City, was in a great location to host friends and relatives going to and from the Mormon temple. They reconnected with old friends and made many new ones through their local church. Mae was not only able to attend meetings at the temple, but also started working with Jennie on genealogy. For her it was the dream of a lifetime. Their lives soon settled into a very pleasant routine. Frank's days, when there was no company, were spent largely in the garden or with the chickens

Excerpts from *Our Home in Draper* by Mary Eliza Roberts Noel (4)

> As I sit and watch my husband
> Working out in the yard,
> Cutting grass and planting roses,

Stepping around without a word,
I know that he is happy
For it is beaming on his face.
And that makes me happy
And I thank God for this place....

We sit and consult quite often
As to how to do this and that.
We laugh and joke and we're happy,
Though seventy, who cares for that?...

Old age is not to be dreaded
If you can meet it as he and I
If your hearts are filled with love
There is nothing to make you cry.
May God ever bless this little spot
With joy and peace and love
That all who ever enter here
Will be thankful to God above.

Their six years in Draper were filled with good memories. In addition to frequent visits, the work in the church and the work in the yard, there were larger celebrations too. Their last year in Draper, they pulled out all the stops for Frank's 80th birthday. The celebration was filled with family and friends and great memories. All Frank asked for was something that all the children could sign. So Newell Scroggins, Bessie's husband, made a beautiful scroll that everyone who was there filled with fond memories. They hung it on their wall so anyone visiting could add to it. They also got their very first set of silverware.

Frank and Mae on his 80th birthday.
Source: Private collection

It wasn't all good obviously. Nothing is ever all good or all bad. There were some health scares. Mae's health continued to deteriorate. She underwent allergy testing and found she was allergic to just about everything. For a while she went in for allergy shots every other day, but, when her health didn't improve, her doctor suggested she just move to a drier climate.

Floyd got her a little apartment in St. George, Utah, about 300 miles from where they lived. There was another Mormon temple there, and she could be near some of her children. But, once again, she was separated from Frank, who had to stay home to care for the chickens. That lasted a few months, about as long as either one could stand it. Frank came to visit in December 1954 and never left.

In March, Mae was advised to move once again, because the pollen was getting bad. According to her report, they came to stay with my family for a couple of weeks in Pueblo, Colorado. My brother and I were toddlers. My father, young Frank, was their twelfth child, and we were from his second marriage. So my grandparents were quite old when we were born.

The author, age 3 and younger brother, Brady picnicking with grandparents.
Source: Private collection.

They ended up buying a little trailer in California, close to where Mary and Chad were living, and settled in for what would be their remaining years. Aware that her health was bad, and not knowing how many more opportunities she would have to talk to everyone, Mae wrote out her final testimony.

Testimony

I may live several years, and I may not; none of us knows when God may see fit to call us home. So, I have decided to add to the little story of my life, before it goes into print, my testimony to the truth of the Gospel. As there are some of my children and some that have joined our family that don't feel just as I feel, there has been little of a religious nature pass between us. Still, I feel a desire, also a duty, to at least leave behind me no doubt as to the way I feel.

I know that the Gospel of Jesus Christ is true, that Joseph Smith was a Prophet of God, that God lives and does hear and answer prayers that are sent to Him in humility, with faith and sincere heart. I have had my prayers answered and I have a burning testimony in my heart that I thank God for.

My sincere prayer is that every one of you will have a desire to get close to your Father in Heaven, that you may enjoy the blessings that his Holy Spirit can give. He can lead you into all truth.

May God bless you to this end, I ask in His holy name.

Amen.
Mary Eliza Roberts Noel (4)

She died April 15, 1957. She was 80 years old.

I have been told that many people believed that, when one of them died, the other would be close behind because their love for each other was so strong. Those people must have forgotten the many times they had to live separately and survive.

When I was in kindergarten, Frank came to stay with us for a month. For a while after Mae died, he just lived one month a year with each of his 13 living children. I remember him being very old, at least from a kindergartener's viewpoint. He was straight and tall and used a cane. Years later, when I was 15, I went to visit my father and he took me to see *his* father. At that point, Frank was no longer able to travel much, and he was living with his oldest daughter, Clara, and her husband. We were invited to stay for dinner, and there was fried chicken and mashed potatoes and a table full of home cooking. Grandpa was quiet. His hearing hadn't been good for a long time, so he may not have heard everything that was going on around him. I was quiet. The family around me seemed loving and glad to be together. But I hadn't been raised with them, and I didn't know them. When Grandpa went off to bed we left.

He died October 31, 1967, at the age of 94.

Together, Frank Leland Noel and Mary Eliza Roberts Noel survived a lot that would have ended other couples: forbidden love, the death of a child, long separations, isolation, poverty, a horrific flood, changing fortunes, a pandemic, the Great Depression, and a Native uprising that was literally resolved in their home.

They also saw many advances. Cars and airplanes became common travel vehicles. No longer would they need to travel 30 miles or more each way in a wagon to get provisions or medical advice. No longer would they need to rent horses in case the cars got stuck in the mud. By the time he died, Frank had become quite comfortable traveling by commercial jet.

Vaccines for tuberculosis and polio were found and widely distributed. Children would not die the way that Frank's parents did… or the way their son did. As a matter of fact, my grandparents—and Hambleton, who was once so sickly his brother didn't recognize him—lived into their 80s and 90s.

During their married life, they saw the inventions of radios, air conditioners, instant coffee and talking motion pictures. They saw the beginning of penicillin, bubble gum, Scotch tape, frozen dinners, stereo records, photocopiers, television, Slinkies, and the aqualung. They would have read about the creation of Einstein's theory of relativity, the atomic bomb, and microwave ovens. (12)

Rooted and established in love and faith, Frank and Mae lived each and every season devoted to each other and their family. When life was good, they celebrated. When it wasn't, they found a way to make it work… together.

CHAPTER 28:

Then and Now

Paynefield: The plantation where Frank was born was sold to Laurence Andrews in 1891 and remained in the Andrews family for many generations. In 2009, it was purchased by Maxie Broaddus with a plan to use a third of the 980 acres for farming. In January 2011, the original house burned down. Flames pictured in the *Rappahannock Times* on January 12 show what some have come to believe is the ghost of Laurence Andrews.

Photo credit: Leslie Thomas Rappahannock Times

The house was rebuilt, and the graveyard behind the house still holds the graves of my great-great grandfather, Edmund Faver Noel, his wife and child, as well as several members of the Andrews family.

Photo credit: Larry Laurita, private collection

In 2015, Maxie Broaddus passed away and his two daughters managed the property, turning it into a popular wedding venue in the area.

In 2022, it was purchased by LloydCoAg LLC, an investment company. I spoke to William Welter there, and he told me Paynefield is still productive agriculturally with crops of corn, wheat, and soybeans. It is also still a gorgeous wedding and event venue with a variety of backdrops available in the main house and barns.

Photo from website-
For more information, or to schedule a visit go to info@paynefieldfarm.com

Two Grey Hills: This name has become synonymous with excellence in Navajo rugs that originate from the Chuska Mountain region of New Mexico. The process used today is the traditional one of carding natural wool fibers without dyes, and weaving them on a loom, just as it was in the first days of Two Grey Hills.

The original Two Grey Hills Trading Post, one of the trading posts owned by Frank and Henry Noel, still operates today, over 100 years later. It is no longer a post where you can purchase flour and sugar but specializes in the creative skills of the Navajo people in the region.

Search Two Grey Hills online and you will find two listings. One is a store in Jackson Hole, Wyoming, where you can find amazing rugs, jewelry, and pottery, sometimes priced into the thousands of dollars.

The other is the original trading post, less accessible, but still operating. At this writing, it is owned by Les Wilson, who says it is usually open when he is there… and he's there most of the time. Just to be sure, you can call ahead. The phone number and directions, that include dirt roads, are posted on the website, which also states, "If the store is closed, rug buyers should drive to the rear and honk persistently." To find the original store, be sure to include the words "trading post" in your search, or just go directly to www.twogreyhills.com.

Two Grey Hills retail in Jackson Hole, Wyoming
Source: picture from website

Sanostee Trading Post has either died or grown into a town. I visited there in 1988. At that point, there was still a trading post and a man who knew of my grandparents. But that was a long time ago.

Today, there is a town by that name in the same area where the trading post was. It contains a school and a post office and an active chapter house of the Navajo nation. The 2010 census shows the total population of Sanostee as 1,795, with 1,781 of the residents being Navajo. However, more recent data shows a population hovering around 300. I spoke to Ora, a very helpful representative at the Sanostee chapter, who told me there had been a trading post near the post office. At one point, it became a video store, but that has closed. There was also a trading post a few miles away, but it is now gone.

Current picture of Sanostee with Beautiful Mountain just behind the buildings.
Picture credit: Ora M. Begay. Red House clan. Mother and father of Many Hogans.

I wondered about the origin of the name, *Sanostee*. Ora said her best guess, and one that makes complete sense, is that the white men couldn't pronounce the Navajo name for the region, and it stuck. *TseAlNaoztii* means "surrounded by canyons."

One thing is true: The Navajo people who befriended Frank and Mae still live, and work, and cherish the land where they were.

If you would like to contact the Sanostee chapter, go to <u>sanostee@ navajochapters.org</u>, or give them a call at 505-723-2702.

Seal of the Sanostee Chapter House of Navajo showing Beautiful Mountain.
Picture provided by Ora M. Begay, Red House clan, Mother and Father of Many Hogans

Beautiful Mountain remains as remote today as it was 125 years ago. And according to The Tony Hillerman Portal of the University of New Mexico, it is just as meaningful to the Navajo people. *Called Dzilk'i IHozhonii (Mountain Beautiful on Top) in Dine', it is the tallest peak in San Juan County, New Mexico and is sacred to the Navajo. It lies 25 miles southwest of Shiprock on the New Mexico – Arizona state line near the Four Corners region. The Navajo believe this mountain is the feet of Goods of Value Mountain, a male spiritual figure. The Navajo believe his legs are the Carrizo Mountains, his body is the Chuska Mountains, his head is the Chuska Peak, and that Shiprock itself is the pouch or weapon he carries.* (13)

Note: *Dine'* is the name the Navajo have for themselves and their language.

Resources

1. **National Park Service**
   About the Homestead Act
   Last modified October 12, 2022
   https://www.nps.gov/home/learn/historyculture/
   abouthomesteadactlaw.htm
   Accessed: June 2022

2. **Tom Perry Special Collection Library**
   BYU Library
   Brigham Young University, Provo Utah

3. *Roberts family: Connecticut to California*
   Hartle, Daphne; Weeks, Jennie N.; and Watkins, Margaret
   Private collection
   Salt Lake City, Utah
   965

4. *80 Years in America*
   Noel, F.L. and Mary E.R.
   Private collection
   Salt Lake City, UT
   1962

5. *Along Navajo Trails: Recollections of a Trader 1898-1948*
   Evans, Will
   University Press of Colorado and Utah State University Press
   April 15, 2005

6. *Book of Remembrance: Noel and Roberts Master Pedigree*
   Compiled by Mary E.R. Noel and Jennie N. Weeks
   Private collection
   Salt Lake City, Utah
   1974

7. *Anselm Weber, O.F.. Missionary to the Navajo* **1898-1921**
   Wilken, Robert L.
   Bruce Publishing Company
   Milwaukee, WI
   1953
   Quoted in "Anselm Weber." *Wikipedia* https://en.wikipedia.org/wiki/Anselm_Weber
   August 2022

8. *River of Lost Souls: The Science, Politics, and Greed Behind the Gold King Mine Disaster*
   Thompson, Jonathan A.
   Torrey House Publishers: Voices for the Land
   First edition
   Salt Lake City, UT
   2018
   Excerpt at https://riveroflostsouls.com/2018/07/23/river-of-lost-souls-excerpt.1911.flood

9. **The Navajo War of 1913**
   Boardman, Mark
   True West Magazine
   June 2013
   https://truewestmagazine.com/article/the-navajo-war-of-1913
   Accessed: August 23, 2022

10. *The Indian Traders*
    McNitt, Frank
    University of Oklahoma Press

First edition
Norman, Oklahoma
1962

11. **Revolt of the Navajo, 1913**
    McKibbin, Davidson B.
    New Mexico Historical Review,
    Vol. 29, #4
    Pages 259-89
    October 1, 1954
    https://digitalrepository.unm.edu/nmhr/vol29/iss4/3/
    Accessed: August 2023

12. **20th Century Invention Timeline 1900 to 1949**
    Bellis, Mary
    ThoughtCo.
    July 31, 2022
    Thoughtco.com/20th-century-timeling-1992486
    Accessed: September 2022

13. **Beautiful Mountain, New Mexico**
    Comerford, Kevin, et al.
    Tony Hillerman Portal
    University of New Mexico Libraries.
    https://ehillerman.unm.edu/node/1097#sthash.butZgWn8.dpbs.
    Accessed: September 2022

www.ingramcontent.com/pod-product-compliance
Ingram Content Group UK Ltd.
Pitfield, Milton Keynes, MK11 3LW, UK
UKHW040615141224
452011UK00001B/23